'Reade him, therefore; and againe, and againe: And if then you do not like him, surely you are in some danger, not to understand him...

John Hemming
Henry Condell

Preface to the 1623 Folio Edition

Shakespeare Made Easy

Titles in the series

Macbeth

Julius Caesar

The Merchant of Venice

Romeo and Juliet

Henry IV Part One

A Midsummer Night's Dream

The Tempest

King Lear

Hamlet

Othello

$8·00

Shakespeare
MADE 'EASY

**Modern version side-by-side with
full original text**

Othello

Edited and rendered into modern English by
Alan Durband

Stanley Thornes (Publishers) Ltd

First published in 1989 by Hutchinson Education

Reprinted 2001 by
Stanley Thornes (Publishers) Ltd
Delta Place
27 Bath Road
CHELTENHAM, GL53 7TH
United Kingdom

04 05 06 07 08 / 10 9 8 7 6 5

British Library Cataloguing in Publication Data

Shakespeare, William, *1564–1616*
    Othello
    I. Title   II. Durband, Alan   III. Series
    IV Series
    822.3'3

    ISBN 0 7487 3358 2

Photoset in Plantin and Helvetica

Printed in Croatia by Zrinski

Contents

Introduction   6
William Shakespeare: life, plays, theatre, verse 8
Othello: date, source, text   14

OTHELLO
Original text and modern version   15

Activities   **290**
Characters   290
Textual questions   306
Examination questions   313
One-word-answer quiz   315
What's missing?   318

Introduction

Shakespeare Made Easy is intended for readers approaching the plays for the first time, who find the language of Elizabethan poetic drama an initial obstacle to understanding and enjoyment. In the past, the only answer to the problem has been to grapple with the difficulties with the aid of explanatory footnotes (often missing when they are most needed) and a stern teacher. Generations of students have complained that 'Shakespeare was ruined for me at school'.

Usually a fuller appreciation of Shakespeare's plays comes in later life, when the mind has matured and language skills are more developed. Often the desire to read Shakespeare for pleasure and enrichment follows from a visit to the theatre, where excellence of acting and production can bring to life qualities which sometimes lie dormant on the printed page.

Shakespeare Made Easy can never be a substitute for the original plays. It cannot possibly convey the full meaning of Shakespeare's poetic expression, which is untranslatable. *Shakespeare Made Easy* concentrates on the dramatic aspect, enabling the novice to become familiar with the plot and characters, and to experience one facet of Shakespeare's genius. To know and understand the central issues of each play is a sound starting point for further exploration and development.

Discretion can be used in choosing the best method to employ. One way is to read the original Shakespeare first, ignoring the modern translation or using it only when interest or understanding flags. Another way is to read the translation first, to establish confidence and familiarity with plots and characters.

Either way, cross-reference can be illuminating. The modern text can explain 'what is being said' if Shakespeare's language is particularly complex or his expression antiquated. The Shakespeare text will show the reader of the modern paraphrase how much more can be expressed in poetry than in prose.

The use of *Shakespeare Made Easy* means that the newcomer need never be overcome by textual difficulties. From first to last, a measure of understanding is at hand – the key is provided for what has been a locked door to many students in the past. And as understanding grows, so an awareness develops of the potential of language as a vehicle for philosophic and moral expression, beauty, and the abidingly memorable.

Even professional Shakespearian scholars can never hope to arrive at a complete understanding of the plays. Each critic, researcher, actor or producer merely adds a little to the work that has already been done, or makes fresh interpretations of the texts for new generations. For everyone, Shakespearian appreciation is a journey. *Shakespeare Made Easy* is intended to help with the first steps.

In the words of Dr Johnson (*Preface to Shakespeare*, 1756): 'I hope I have made my author's meaning accessible to many who before were frightened from perusing him.'

Alan Durband

William Shakespeare

His life

William Shakespeare was born in Stratford-on-Avon, Warwickshire, on 23 April 1564, the son of a prosperous wool and leather merchant. Very little is known of his early life. From parish records we know that he married Ann Hathaway in 1582, when he was eighteen, and she was twenty-six. They had three children, the eldest of whom died in childhood.

Between his marriage and the next thing we know about him, there is a gap of ten years. Probably he became a member of a travelling company of actors. By 1592 he had settled in London, and had earned a reputation as an actor and playwright.

Theatres were then in their infancy. The first (called *The Theatre*) was built by the actor James Burbage in 1576, in Shoreditch, then a suburb of London. Two more followed as the taste for theatre grew: *The Curtain* in 1577 and *The Rose* in 1587. The demand for new plays naturally increased. Shakespeare probably earned a living adapting old plays and working in collaboration with others on new ones. Today we would call him a 'freelance', since he was not permanently attached to one theatre.

In 1594, a new company of actors, The Lord Chamberlain's Men was formed, and Shakespeare was one of the shareholders. He remained a member throughout his working life. The Company was regrouped in 1603, and re-named The King's Men, with James I as their patron.

Shakespeare and his fellow-actors prospered. In 1598 they built their own theatre, *The Globe*, which broke away from the traditional rectangular shape of the inn and its yard (the early home of travelling bands of actors). Shakespeare described it in *Henry V* as 'this wooden O', because it was circular.

Many other theatres were built by investors eager to profit from the new enthusiasm for drama. *The Hope, The Fortune, The Red Bull,* and *The Swan* were all open-air 'public' theatres. There were also many 'private' (or indoor) theatres, one of which (*The Blackfriars*) was purchased by Shakespeare and his friends because the child actors who performed there were dangerous competitors (Shakespeare denounces them in *Hamlet*).

After writing some thirty-seven plays (the exact number is something which scholars argue about), Shakespeare retired to his native Stratford, wealthy and respected. He died on his birthday, in 1616.

His plays

Shakespeare's plays were not all published in his lifetime. None of them comes to us exactly as he wrote it.

In Elizabethan times, plays were not regarded as either literature or good reading matter. They were written at speed (often by more than one writer), performed perhaps ten or twelve times, and then discarded. Fourteen of Shakespeare's plays were first printed in Quarto (17cm × 21cm) volumes, not all with his name as the author. Some were authorized (the 'good' Quartos) and probably were printed from prompt copies provided by the theatre. Others were pirated (the 'bad' Quartos) by booksellers who may have employed shorthand writers, or bought actors' copies after the run of the play had ended.

In 1623, seven years after Shakespeare's death, John Hemming and Henry Condell (fellow-actors and shareholders in The King's Men) published a collected edition of Shakespeare's works – thirty-six plays in all – in a Folio (21cm × 34cm) edition. From their introduction it would seem that they used Shakespeare's original manuscripts ('we have scarce received from him a blot in his papers') but the Folio volumes that still survive are not all exactly alike, nor are the plays printed as we know them today, with act and scene divisions and stage-directions.

A modern edition of a Shakespeare play is the result of a great deal of scholarly research and editorial skill over several centuries. The aim is always to publish a text (based on the good and bad Quartos and the Folio editions) that most closely resembles what Shakespeare intended. Misprints have added to the problems, so some words and lines are pure guesswork. This explains why some versions of Shakespeare's plays differ from others.

His theatre

The first purpose-built playhouse in Elizabethan London, constructed in 1576, was *The Theatre*. Its co-founders were John Brayne, an investor, and James Burbage, a carpenter turned actor. Like the six or seven 'public' (or outdoor) theatres which followed it over the next thirty years, it was situated outside the city, to avoid conflict with the authorities. They disapproved of players and playgoing, partly on moral and political grounds, and partly because of the danger of spreading the plague. (There were two major epidemics during Shakespeare's lifetime, and on each occasion the theatres were closed for lengthy periods.)

The Theatre was a financial success, and Shakespeare's company performed there until 1598, when a dispute over the lease of the land forced Burbage to take down the building. It was recreated in Southwark, as *The Globe*, with Shakespeare and several of his fellow-actors as the principal shareholders.

By modern standards, *The Globe* was small. Externally, the octagonal building measured less than thirty metres across, but in spite of this it could accommodate an audience of between two and three thousand people. (The largest of the three theatres at the National Theatre complex in London today seats 1160.)

Performances were advertised by means of playbills posted around the city, and they took place during the hours of daylight when the weather was suitable. A flag flew to show that all was well, to save playgoers a wasted journey.

At the entrance, a doorkeeper collected one penny (about 60p in modern money) for admission to the 'pit' – a name taken from the old inn-yards, where bear-baiting and cock-fighting were popular sports. This was the minimum charge for seeing a play. The 'groundlings', as they were called, simply stood around the three sides of the stage, in the open air. Those who were better off could pay extra for a seat under cover. Stairs led from the pit to three tiers of galleries round the walls. The higher one went, the more one paid. The best seats cost one shilling, (or £6 today). In theatres owned by speculators like Francis Langley and Philip Henslowe, half the gallery takings went to the landlord.

A full house might consist of 800 groundlings and 1500 in the galleries, with a dozen more exclusive seats on the stage itself for the gentry. A new play might run for between six and sixteen performances; the average was about ten. As there were no breaks between scenes, and no intervals, most plays could be performed in two hours. A trumpet sounded three times before the play began.

The acting company assembled in the Tiring House at the rear of the stage. This was where they 'attired' (or dressed) themselves: not in costumes representing the period of the play, but in Elizabethan doublet and hose. All performances were therefore in modern dress, though no expense was spared to make the stage costumes lavish. The entire company was male. By law actresses were not allowed, and female roles were performed by boys.

Access to the stage from the Tiring House was through two doors, one on each side of the stage. Because there was no

11

front curtain, every entrance had to have its corresponding exit, so an actor killed on stage had to be carried off. There was no scenery: the audience used its imagination, guided by the spoken word. Storms and night scenes might well be performed on sunny days in mid-afternoon; the Elizabethan playgoer relied entirely on the playwrights' descriptive skills to establish the dramatic atmosphere.

Once on stage, the actors and their expensive clothes were protected from sudden showers by a canopy, the underside of which was painted blue, and spangled with stars to represent the heavens. A trapdoor in the stage made ghostly entrances and the gravedigging scene in *Hamlet* possible. Behind the main stage, in between the two entrance doors, there was a curtained area, concealing a small inner stage, useful for bedroom scenes. Above this was a balcony, which served for castle walls (as in *Henry V*) or a domestic balcony (as in the famous scene in *Romeo and Juliet*).

The acting style in Elizabethan times was probably more declamatory than we favour today, but the close proximity of the audience also made a degree of intimacy possible. In those days soliloquies and asides seemed quite natural. Act and scene divisions did not exist (those in printed versions of the play today have been added by editors), but Shakespeare often indicates a scene-ending by a rhyming couplet.

A company such as The King's Men at *The Globe* would consist of around twenty-five actors, half of whom might be shareholders, and the rest part-timers engaged for a particular play. Amongst the shareholders in *The Globe* were several specialists – William Kempe, for example, was a renowned comedian and Robert Armin was a singer and dancer. Playwrights wrote parts to suit the actors who were available, and devised ways of overcoming the absence of women. Shakespeare often has his heroines dress as young men, and physical contact between lovers was formal compared with the realism we expect today.

His verse

Shakespeare wrote his plays mostly in blank verse: that is, unrhymed lines consisting of ten syllables, alternately stressed and unstressed. The technical term for this form is the 'iambic pentameter'. When Shakespeare first began to write for the stage, it was fashionable to maintain this regular beat from the first line of the play till the last.

Shakespeare conformed at first, and then experimented. Some of his early plays contain whole scenes in rhyming couplets – in *Romeo and Juliet*, for example, there is extensive use of rhyme, and as if to show his versatility, Shakespeare even inserts a sonnet into the dialogue.

But as he matured, he sought greater freedom of expression than rhyme allowed. Rhyme is still used to indicate a scene-ending, or to stress lines which he wishes the audience to remember. Generally, though, Shakespeare moved towards the rhythms of everyday speech. This gave him many dramatic advantages, which he fully and subtly exploits in terms of atmosphere, character, emotion, stress and pace.

It is Shakespeare's poetic imagery, however, that most distinguishes his verse from that of lesser playwrights. It enables him to stretch the imagination, express complex thought-patterns in memorable language, and convey a number of associated ideas in a compressed and economical form. A study of Shakespeare's imagery -- especially in his later plays – is often the key to a full understanding of his meaning and purposes.

At the other extreme is prose. Shakespeare normally reserves it for servants, clowns, commoners, and pedestrian matters such as lists, messages and letters.

Othello

Date

We know from the Revels Account that *Othello* was performed at Court in 1604, by which time it must already have been a success in the theatre. Shakespeare probably wrote the play two or three years earlier, but the exact date is not known.

Source

There is no doubt that the story of Othello comes from a collection called the *Hecatommithi* ('The Hundred Tales') which was written by an Italian, Giraldi Cinthio, in 1566, and translated into French in 1584. It seems likely that Shakespeare also used translations of Pliny's *Natural History* and Cardinal Contarino's *Commonwealth and Government of Venice* during his preparatory research. As usual, Shakespeare radically reworks the borrowed plot to suit his dramatic purposes; the play dwarfs the prose story into insignificance.

Text

Othello was first published in a Quarto version six years after Shakespeare's death. A year later, in 1623, the Folio edition appeared. As the Folio contains approximately 160 lines more than the Quarto, most scholars favour it. However, there are lines in the Quarto that are not in the Folio, and oaths and blasphemies are stronger in the former than in the latter. Consequently, every edition of *Othello* is different as each editor has to make choices. The present edition errs on the side of completeness and colloquial vigour.

Othello

Original text and modern version

The characters

The Duke of Venice
Brabantio   a Venetian senator and Desdemona's father
Gratiano   Brabantio's brother
Lodovico   a relative of Brabantio
Othello   a Moor; in command of the Venetian army
Cassio   his Lieutenant
Iago   his staff-sergeant
Roderigo   a Venetian gentleman, in love with Desdemona
Montano   Governor of Cyprus before Othello
Desdemona   Brabantio's daughter, and Othello's wife
Emilia   Iago's wife
Bianca   Cassio's mistress

**Senators of Venice, Gentlemen of Cyprus, Sailors,
Musicians, Officers, a Messenger, a Herald, a Clown,
Attendants, Soldiers and Servants**

Act one

Scene 1

Venice. A street. Enter **Roderigo** *and* **Iago**.

Roderigo   Tush, never tell me! I take it much unkindly
That thou, Iago, who hast had my purse
As if the strings were thine, shouldst know of this.

Iago   'Sblood, but you will not hear me!
5   If ever I did dream of such a matter,
Abhor me.

Roderigo   Thou told'st me thou didst hold him in thy hate.

Iago   Despise me if I do not. Three great ones of the city,
In personal suit to make me his Lieutenant,
10   Off-capped to him: and by the faith of man,
I know my price, I am worth no worse a place.
But he, as loving his own pride and purposes,
Evades them with a bombast circumstance
Horribly stuffed with epithets of war;
15   And in conclusion,
Non-suits my mediators. For 'Certes,' says he,
'I have already chose my officer.'
And what was he?
Forsooth, a great arithmetician,
20   One Michael Cassio, a Florentine –
A fellow almost damned in a fair wife –
That never set a squadron in the field,
Nor the division of a battle knows
More than a spinster – unless the bookish theoric,
25   Wherein the tongued consuls can propose

Act one

Scene 1

Evening, in a street outside the house of Brabantio, a Venetian senator. **Roderigo,** *a man easily duped, and* **Iago,** *a devious manipulator, are in animated conversation about* **Othello,** *a Moor and Commander of the Venetian Army.*

Roderigo Oh, don't tell me that! It galls me that you should know of this, Iago, having had the freedom of my purse!

Iago Damn it, you won't listen to me! Never speak to me again if I ever dreamt of such a thing!

Roderigo You told me you hated him!

Iago Despise me if I don't. Three of the city's VIPs went cap in hand, personally, to back me as his lieutenant. 'Strewth: I know my price! I'm worth no less! Cock-sure and liking his own way – he dodges them with a load of military claptrap. In the end he turns my backers down. 'It so happens,' says he, 'I have already chosen my First Officer.' And who was that? D'you know, a great theory-man: one Michael Cassio, a Florentine; a fellow with a pretty wife, to his peril. He's never seen action, and he knows no more about tactics than an old maid – apart from academic theory, in which matters the prattling

As masterly as he. Mere prattle without practice
Is all his soldiership. But he, sir, had the election:
And I, of whom his eyes had seen the proof
At Rhodes, at Cyprus, and on other grounds
30   Christian and heathen, must be be-lee'd and calmed
By debitor and creditor; this counter-caster,
He, in good time, must his Lieutenant be,
And I – God bless the mark! – his Moorship's Ancient.

Roderigo   By heaven, I rather would have been his
35   hangman.

Iago   But there's no remedy. 'Tis the curse of service:
Preferment goes by letter and affection,
And not by old gradation, where each second
Stood heir to the first. Now, sir, be judge yourself
40   Whether I in any just term am affined
To love the Moor.

Roderigo   I would not follow him then.

Iago   Oh, sir, content you.
I follow him to serve my turn upon him.
45   We cannot all be masters, nor all masters
Cannot be truly followed. You shall mark
Many a duteous and knee-crooking knave
That, doting on his own obsequious bondage,
Wears out his time, much like his master's ass,
50   For nought but provender; and when he's old –
cashiered!
Whip me such honest knaves. Others there are
Who, trimmed in forms and visages of duty,
Keep yet their hearts attending on themselves,
55   And, throwing but shows of service on their lords,
Do well thrive by them; and when they have lined their
coats,
Do themselves homage. These fellows have some soul,

politicians can speak with as much authority as he. 'All talk and no experience' sums up his soldiership. But he, sir, got the job. And I, whose worth he'd seen with his own eyes at Rhodes, at Cyprus and other Christian and heathen countries – I'm left standing by a rule-book man! This armchair theorist, he gets to be his Lieutenant, and I – for God's sake! – only His Moorship's staff-sergeant.

Roderigo   By heaven, I'd rather be his hangman!

Iago   There's no point in complaining. It's the curse of government service. Promotion goes by influence and who you know, not by seniority, with one rank leading naturally to the next. So, sir: judge for yourself whether by any stretch of the imagination I'm obliged to love the Moor.

Roderigo   I wouldn't serve under him, then.

Iago   Oh, dear sir, rest assured! I serve him to get my revenge. We cannot all be leaders, nor can all leaders be faithfully followed. There's many a dutiful and grovelling wretch who works all his life, loving his own boot-licking slavery, for no more than his grub – just like his master's ass. When he's old – the knacker's! Creeps like that want whipping. Then there are the others: experts in acting and looking dutiful. They look after number one. And though their service is only a sham, they prosper. In lining their own pockets, they keep their self-respect. These fellows have guts, and I reckon I'm

And such a one do I profess myself.
60   For, sir,
It is as sure as you are Roderigo,
Were I the Moor, I would not be Iago:
In following him, I follow but myself.
Heaven is my judge, not I for love and duty,
65   But seeming so for my peculiar end:
For when my outward action doth demonstrate
The native act and figure of my heart
In compliment extern, 'tis not long after,
But I will wear my heart upon my sleeve
70   For daws to peck at. I am not what I am.

Roderigo   What a full fortune does the thick-lips owe
If he can carry't thus!

Iago   Call up her father.
Rouse him, make after him, poison his delight,
75   Proclaim him in the streets; incense her kinsmen,
And, though he in a fertile climate dwell,
Plague him with flies: though that his joy be joy,
Yet throw such chances of vexation on't,
As it may lose some colour.

80   **Roderigo**   Here is her father's house. I'll call aloud.

Iago   Do, with like timorous accent and dire yell,
As when, by night and negligence, the fire
Is spied in populous cities.

Roderigo   What, ho, Brabantio! Signor Brabantio, ho!

85   **Iago**   Awake! What, ho, Brabantio! Thieves, thieves!
Look to your house, your daughter, and your bags!
Thieves! Thieves!

[**Brabantio** *appears above, at a window*]

one of them. Because, sir, it's as certain as you are Roderigo that if I were the Moor, I would not be the man I am. In serving him, I keep my integrity. Love and duty are for heaven to judge, not me. I pretend to be loyal because it suits my purposes. If ever my outward behaviour reveals the real me, then I'll soon start wearing my heart on my sleeve too, for jackdaws to peck at! I am not the man I seem to be . . .

Roderigo   What marvellous luck for the darkie if he can get away with it! [*He is referring to* **Othello** *and his marriage to* **Desdemona,** *the daughter of Brabantio*]

Iago   Summon her father; wake Othello up; follow him around; ruin his pleasure; denounce him in public. Stir things up with her family. Though he's got everything going for him, pester him with irritations. Though he's over the moon, needle him and take the smile off his face.

Roderigo   Here's her father's house. I'll make a rumpus.

Iago   Do. Put the fear of God into them, like finding fire in a crowded city!

Roderigo   Brabantio! Signor Brabantio!

Iago   Hey there! Brabantio! Thieves! Thieves! Watch out for your house, your daughter, and your money! Thieves! Thieves!

[**Brabantio** *appears at the upstairs window*]

Brabantio   What is the reason of this terrible summons?
What is the matter there?

90 **Roderigo**   Signor, is all your family within?

Iago   Are all doors locked?

Brabantio   Why, wherefore ask you this?

Iago   Zounds, sir, you're robbed. For shame, put on your
gown;
95   Your heart is burst, you have lost half your soul.
Even now, now, very now, an old black ram
Is tupping your white ewe. Arise, arise,
Awake the snoring citizens with the bell,
Or else the devil will make a grandsire of you.
100   Arise, I say!

Brabantio   What, have you lost your wits?

Roderigo   Most reverend signor, do you know my voice?

Brabantio   Not I: what are you?

Roderigo   My name is Roderigo.

105 **Brabantio**   The worser welcome!
I have charged thee not to haunt about my doors.
In honest plainness thou hast heard me say
My daughter is not for thee. And now in madness,
Being full of supper and distempering draughts,
110   Upon malicious knavery dost thou come
To start my quiet?

Roderigo   Sir, sir, sir –

Brabantio   But thou must needs be sure
My spirit and my place have in them power
115   To make this bitter to thee.

Roderigo   Patience, good sir.

Brabantio What's all this hullabaloo? What's the matter?

Roderigo Signor, is all your family at home?

Iago Are all your doors locked?

Brabantio Why do you ask?

Iago Dammit, you've been robbed. For decency's sake, put your dressing-gown on. Your heart has been broken; you've lost half your soul. Now, now, right now, an old black ram is having it off with your white ewe! Get up, get up! Ring the bell and rouse the snoring citizens, or the devil will make a grandfather of you! Get up, will you?

Brabantio What, have you lost your wits?

Roderigo Most respected Signor: do you recognize my voice?

Brabantio I don't. Who are you?

Roderigo My name's Roderigo.

Brabantio All the worse for that! I've told you not to haunt my doors. You've heard me say quite plainly that my daughter is not for you. And now, full of drink and Dutch courage, have you come here out of sheer villainy to make a disturbance?

Roderigo Sir, sir, sir –

Brabantio Be assured I have the means and the will to make you regret this!

Roderigo Calm yourself, good sir –

Brabantio   What tell'st thou me of robbing? This is
   Venice:
   My house is not a grange.

120 **Roderigo**   Most grave Brabantio,
   In simple and pure soul I come to you . . .

Iago   Zounds, sir, you are one of those that will not serve
   God if the devil bid you. Because we come to do you
   service and you think we are ruffians, you'll have your
125   daughter covered with a Barbary horse; you'll have your
   nephews neigh to you, you'll have coursers for cousins,
   and jennets for germans.

Brabantio   What profane wretch art thou?

Iago   I am one, sir, that comes to tell you, your daughter
130   and the Moor are now making the beast with two backs.

Brabantio   Thou art a villian.

Iago   You are – a Senator.

Brabantio   This thou shalt answer. I know thee, Roderigo.

Roderigo   Sir, I will answer anything. But I beseech you
135   If't be your pleasure and most wise consent,
   As partly I find it is, that your fair daughter,
   At this odd-even and dull watch o'th'night,
   Transported with no worse nor better guard
   But with a knave of common hire, a gondolier,
140   To the gross clasps of a lascivious Moor –
   If this be known to you, and your allowance,
   We then have done you bold and saucy wrongs;
   But if you know not this, my manners tell me
   We have your wrong rebuke. Do not believe
145   That from the sense of all civility
   I thus would play and trifle with your reverence.

Brabantio   What's all this about burglary? This is
Venice. I don't live out in the country.

Roderigo   Most respected Brabantio, I come to you in
all sincerity and honesty –

Iago   Dammit, sir, you're one of those people who'd
deny God if the devil told you to worship him.
Because we come to do you a favour, you think we
are ruffians. You'll let your daughter be mated with
a black stallion: you'll have your grandchildren
neighing to you; your cousins will be hunters; you'll
have ponies for your near relations!

Brabantio   What kind of foul-mouthed wretch are
you?

Iago   I've come to tell you, sir, that your daughter and
the Moor are having it off.

Brabantio   You are a villain!

Iago   You are – [*he avoids abuse*] a Senator –

Brabantio   You'll answer for this! I know you,
Roderigo!

Roderigo   Sir, I'll answer any charges. But may I ask
whether it is your wish and with your consent – as I
suspect it is – that your beautiful daughter, in the
early hours of the morning, should be conveyed by
no worse and no better guard than a mere hired
servant – a gondolier – to the lusty arms of a
lascivious Moor? If you know about it, and it has
your permission, then we have wronged you
outrageously and insolently. But if you don't know,
manners tell me we've been wrongly rebuked. Don't
think I would play and trifle with Your Reverence so

Your daughter, if you have not given her leave,
I say again, hath made a gross revolt,
Tying her duty, beauty, wit, and fortunes
150 In an extravagant and wheeling stranger
Of here and everywhere. Straight satisfy yourself:
If she be in her chamber or your house,
Let loose on me the justice of the state
For thus deluding you.

155 **Brabantio**   Strike on the tinder, ho!
Give me a taper! Call up all my people!
This accident is not unlike my dream:
Belief of it oppresses me already.
Light, I say, light!

[Exit above]

160 **Iago**   Farewell, for I must leave you.
It seems not meet, nor wholesome to my place,
To be produced – as if I stay, I shall –
Against the Moor. For I do know the state,
However this may gall him with some check,
165 Cannot with safety cast him; for he's embarked
With such loud reason to the Cyprus wars,
Which even now stand in act, that for their souls
Another of his fathom they have none
To lead their business. In which regard,
170 Though I do hate him as I do hell's pains,
Yet for necessity of present life
I must show out a flag and sign of love,
Which is indeed but sign. That you shall surely find
him,
175 Lead to the Sagittary the raised search;
And there will I be with him. So farewell.

[Exit]

uncivilly. I say again, if you haven't given her permission, then your daughter has transgressed most shamefully. Her duty, beauty, common-sense and future prospects are all tied up with an unknown vagabond. Settle your mind right now. If she's in her bedroom or your house, have the law on me for deluding you like this!

Brabantio Lights, there! Give me a taper! Rouse the household! This is like a dream. It depresses me to realise it's not. Light, I say, light!

[*He disappears inside*]

Iago I must go now: goodbye. It wouldn't be right nor helpful to my career to be a witness against the Moor, which I shall be if I stay. Though he might be reprimanded, Venice cannot with safety sack him. By common consent he is to command the Cyprus wars that are now in full swing, and they haven't anyone else of his calibre to take over. So, though I hate him like the torments of hell, it's vital at the present time to make a gesture, a sign of loyalty, which is indeed no more than that. Lead the search party to the Arrow Inn — you'll find him there for sure. I'll be with him. Goodbye.

[*He goes*]

(*Enter below* **Brabantio** *in his night-gown with servants and torches*)

Brabantio   It is too true an evil. Gone she is,
And what's to come of my despised time
Is naught but bitterness. Now, Roderigo,
180   Where didst thou see her? Oh, unhappy girl! –
With the Moor, say'st thou? Who would be a father? –
How didst thou know 'twas she? Oh, she deceives me
Past thought! What said she to you? Get more tapers!
Raise all my kindred! Are they married, think you?

185 **Roderigo**   Truly I think they are.

Brabantio   Oh heaven! How got she out? Oh treason of
the blood!
Fathers, from hence trust not your daughters' minds
By what you see them act. Is there not charms
190   By which the property of youth and maidhood
May be abused? Have you not read, Roderigo,
Of some such thing?

Roderigo   Yes, sir, I have indeed.

Brabantio   Call up my brother. Oh, would you had had
195   her!
Some one way, some another. Do you know
Where we may apprehend her and the Moor?

Roderigo   I think I can discover him, if you please
To get good guard and go along with me.

200 **Brabantio**   Pray you, lead on. At every house I'll call –
I may command at most. Get weapons, ho!
And raise some special officers of night.
On, good Roderigo; I'll deserve your pains.

[*Exeunt*]

[**Brabantio** *enters in his dressing gown, with servants carrying torches*]

Brabantio   It's all too wickedly true. She is gone. The rest of my miserable life will be nothing but bitterness. Now, Roderigo, where did you see her? Oh, unhappy girl! With the Moor, did you say? Who would be a father! How did you know it was she? Oh, you have deceived me unthinkably! What did she say to you? Get more lights! Summon all my kinfolk. Are they married, do you think?

Roderigo   Indeed I think they are.

Brabantio   Oh, god! How did she get out? Oh, this passion! Fathers, henceforth do not judge your daughters' minds by what you see them do. Are there not magic charms that can work upon young people and maidens? Haven't you read of some such things, Roderigo?

Roderigo   Yes sir, I have indeed.

Brabantio   [*To Servants*] Waken my brother. [*To Roderigo*] I wish she'd been yours now! [*To more Servants*] Some go one way, some another. [*To Roderigo*] Do you know where we can catch her and the Moor?

Roderigo   I think I can find him, if you'd be good enough to arrange for an escort, and come with me.

Brabantio   Lead the way, I'll stop at every house. I have influence with most. [*To Servants*] Get weapons, will you? Get the special night patrol. Proceed, good Roderigo. I'm obliged to you.

[*They go*]

Scene 2

Enter **Othello**, **Iago** *and attendants with torches.*

Iago Though in the trade of war I have slain men,
    Yet do I hold it very stuff of the conscience
    To do no contrived murder: I lack iniquity
    Sometimes to do me service. Nine or ten times
5   I had thought to have yerked him here under the ribs.

Othello 'Tis better as it is.

Iago   Nay, but he prated
    And spoke such scurvy and provoking terms
    Against your honour,
10   That with the little godliness I have,
    I did full hard forbear him. But I pray you, sir,
    Are you fast married? Be assured of this,
    That the Magnifico is much beloved,
    And hath in his effect a voice potential
15   As double as the Duke's. He will divorce you,
    Or put upon you what restraint and grievance
    That law, with all his might to enforce it on,
    Will give him cable.

Othello   Let him do his spite:
20   My services, which I have done the signory,
    Shall out-tongue his complaints. 'Tis yet to know –
    Which, when I know that boasting is an honour,
    I shall promulgate – I fetch my life and being
    From men of royal siege, and my demerits
25   May speak unbonneted to as proud a fortune
    As this that I have reached. For know, Iago,
    But that I love the gentle Desdemona,
    I would not my unhoused free condition
    Put into circumscription and confine
30   For the seas' worth. But look, what lights come yonder?

32

Scene 2

Othello *the Moor enters, followed by* **Iago** *and Attendants carrying torches.*

Iago   I've killed men in wartime, but my conscience jibs at cold-blooded murder. I'm too scrupulous for my own good. Nine or ten times I've thought I might stab him here under the ribs.

Othello   It's better as it is.

Iago   Yes, but he shot his mouth off and spoke so disparagingly against your honour that it was a hard struggle to let it pass, me being no saint. But are you legally married, may I presume to ask? Because you can be sure of this: Signor Brabantio, the Magnifico, is very well liked, and has powerful influence, every bit the equal of the Duke's. He will divorce you, or constrain and hassle you as far as his powerful command of the law will allow.

Othello   Let him do his worst. My services to the Venetian Government will speak more eloquently than his complaints. It is not generally known (when boasting is honourable I might make it public) that I come from men of royal status, and my rank is the proud equal of what I have achieved here. I tell you, Iago: if it were not that I love the gentle Desdemona, I would not limit my freedom and independence for all the treasure in the sea. [*He sees the approaching search party*] But look – whose lights are those?

Iago   Those are the raised father and his friends:
You were best go in.

Othello   Not I: I must be found.
My parts, my title, and my perfect soul
35   Shall manifest me rightly, Is it they?

Iago   By Janus, I think no.

[*Enter* **Cassio,** *with officers bearing torches*]

Othello   The servants of the Duke and my Lieutenant!
The goodness of the night upon you, friends!
What is the news?

40 **Cassio**   The Duke does greet you, General,
And he requires your haste-post-haste appearance
Even on the instant.

Othello   What is the matter, think you?

Cassio   Something from Cyprus, as I may divine:
45   It is a business of some heat. The galleys
Have sent a dozen sequent messengers
This very night at one another's heels;
And many of the consuls, raised and met,
Are at the Duke's already. You have been hotly called
50   for,
When being not at your lodging to be found.
The senate hath sent about three several quests
To search you out.

Othello   'Tis well I am found by you:
55   I will but spend a word here in the house
And go with you.

                                                    [*Exit*]

Cassio   Ancient, what makes he here?

Iago   It's the father and his friends who've been awakened. You'd better go in.

Othello   Not I. I must be available. My character, my rank, and my integrity will justly speak for me. Are they the ones?

Iago   By Janus [*Janus was a two-faced god*] I don't think so –

[**Michael Cassio, Othello's** *Lieutenant, enters with men carrying torches*]

Othello   Some servants of the Duke, and my Lieutenant! Good evening to you, friends. What news?

Cassio   The Duke greets you, General, and demands to see you now, immediately.

Othello   About what?

Cassio   Something from Cyprus as far as I can tell. It's urgent. The navy has sent a dozen messengers this very night one after the other. Many of the senators are up and at the Duke's, having already conferred. They needed you urgently, and when they couldn't find you at your lodgings, the senate sent out three separate search-parties to look for you.

Othello   It's as well you found me. I'll just have a word inside the house, then go with you.

[*He goes indoors*]

Cassio   Sergeant, what is he doing here?

Iago   Faith, he tonight hath boarded a land carrack:
          If it prove lawful prize, he's made for ever.

60 **Cassio**   I do not understand.

Iago   He's married.

Cassio   To who?

Iago   Marry, to – Come, Captain, will you go?

          [*Enter* **Othello**]

Othello   Have with you.

65 **Cassio**   Here comes another troop to seek for you.

          (*Enter* **Brabantio, Roderigo,** *and officers with torches*)

Iago   It is Brabantio. General, be advised,
          He comes to bad intent.

Othello   Holla, stand there!

Roderigo   Signor, it is the Moor.

70 **Brabantio**   Down with him, thief!

          [*They draw on both sides*]

Iago   You, Roderigo, come sir, I am for you.

Othello   Keep up your bright swords, for the dew will rust
          them.
          Good signor, you shall more command with years
75   Than with your weapons.

Brabantio   Oh thou foul thief! Where has thou stowed my
          daughter?
          Damned as thou art, thou hast enchanted her:
          For I'll refer me to all things of sense,
80   If she in chains of magic were not bound,
          Whether a maid, so tender, fair, and happy,

Iago 'Strewth, he's captured a real treasure-ship tonight. If it's all above board, he's made forever.

Cassio I don't get you.

Iago He's married.

Cassio Who to?

Iago Why, to – [**Othello** *returns*] Come, Captain: are you ready?

Othello I'm with you.

Cassio Here's another troop looking for you.

[**Brabantio, Roderigo,** *and Officers carrying torches, enter*]

Iago It's Brabantio. General, take my advice. He's here to make trouble.

Othello Hold it there!

Roderigo [*to* **Brabantio**] Signor, it is the Moor.

Brabantio Down with him, the thief!

Iago [*to* **Roderigo**] You, Roderigo. [*He draws his sword*] Come on, sir, I'm ready for you!

Othello Sheath your bright swords or the dew will rust them! [*To* **Brabantio**] Good Signor, your age commands more respect than your weapons.

Brabantio Oh you foul thief! Where have you hidden my daughter? Damned as you are, you've cast a spell on her. I ask anyone or anything with a scrap of intelligence: if she wasn't the prisoner of a magic spell, would a maiden who's so gentle, beautiful

So opposite to marriage that she shunned
The wealthy curled darlings of our nation,
Would ever have, to incur a general mock,
85 Run from her guardage to the sooty bosom
Of such a thing as thou: to fear, not to delight.
Judge me the world, if 'tis not gross in sense
That thou hast practised on her with foul charms,
Abused her delicate youth with drugs or minerals
90 That weakens motion. I'll have't disputed on;
'Tis probable, and palpable to thinking:
I therefore apprehend, and do attach thee
For an abuser of the world, a practiser
Of arts inhibited, and out of warrant.
95 Lay hold upon him: if he do resist,
Subdue him, at his peril!

Othello   Hold your hands,
Both you of my inclining, and the rest.
Were it my cue to fight, I should have known it
100 Without a prompter. Where will you that I go
To answer this your charge?

Brabantio   To prison, till fit time
Of law and course of direct session
Call thee to answer.

105 **Othello**   What if I do obey?
How may the Duke be therewith satisfied,
Whose messengers are here about my side,
Upon some present business of the state
To bring me to him?

110 **1st Officer**   'Tis true, most worthy signor:
The Duke's in council, and your noble self
I am sure is sent for.

and happy, and so opposed to marriage that she shunned the most wealthy and handsome eligible bachelors of our nation – would she ever have invited public ridicule by running away from her father's home into the sooty arms of such a man as you? One to be frightened of – not love. Let the world decide if it isn't obvious that you have practised sorcery on her, and corrupted her tender young body with drugs or poisons that weaken the faculties. I'll have it investigated. It's very probable, and makes sense: I therefore hold and arrest you as a corrupter of the world, a practiser of banned and intolerable black arts. Seize him! If he resists, use whatever force is necessary.

Othello Make no move – neither my men nor yours. If it were a fighting matter, I'd need no prompting. Where do you wish me to go to answer this charge of yours?

Brabantio To prison, till the law is ready to deal with you, and the court is in session to hear you defend yourself.

Othello What if I obey? How can I at the same time satisfy the Duke, whose messengers are here at my side to take me to him on urgent state business?

1st Officer It is true, most worthy Signor. The Duke is in council, and I'm sure your noble self has been sent for.

Brabantio   How? The Duke in council?
In this time of the night? Bring him away.
115   Mine's not an idle cause; the Duke himself,
Or any of my brothers of the state,
Cannot but feel this wrong as 'twere their own;
For if such actions may have passage free,
Bondslaves and pagans shall our statesmen be.

[*Exeunt*]

Scene 3

A Council-chamber. The **Duke** *and Senators sitting at a table;
with lights and attendants.*

Duke   There is no composition in these news
That gives them credit.

1st Senator   Indeed they are disproportioned.
My letters say a hundred and seven galleys.

5   **Duke**   And mine a hundred and forty.

2nd Senator   And mine two hundred;
But though they jump not on a just account
As in these cases where the aim reports
'Tis oft with difference – yet do they all confirm
10   A Turkish fleet, and bearing up to Cyprus.

Duke   Nay, it is possible enough to judgement:
I do not so secure me in the error,
But the main article I do approve
In fearful sense.

15   **Sailor**   [*within*] What, ho! What, ho! What, ho!

Brabantio   What? The Duke in council? At this time of the night? Take him away. Mine's not a trivial issue. The Duke himself, or any of my peers, could not but feel this wrong as if it were their own. If such behaviour goes unchecked, one day slaves and pagans will take over the government.

[*They go*]

Scene 3

The **Duke** *and the* **Senators** *are in session, attended by Officials and Servants carrying lights.*

Duke   There is no consistency in these despatches to give them credence.

1st Senator   Indeed, the figures don't match. My letters say 'A hundred and seven' galleys.

Duke   And mine, 'a hundred and forty'.

2nd Senator   And mine 'two hundred'. But though they don't tally arithmetically – estimates always vary in these circumstances – yet nevertheless they all confirm the existence of a Turkish fleet, and that it's approaching Cyprus.

Duke   Yes, it all points to the same thing. The factual differences give me no reason to feel secure: I take the main point and its frightening implications.

Sailor   [*shouting from outside*] Hello there! Hello there! Hello there!

1st Officer   A messenger from the galleys.

(*Enter a* **Sailor**)

Duke   Now, what's the business?

Sailor   The Turkish preparation makes for Rhodes;
So was I bid report here to the state
20   By Signor Angelo.

Duke   How say you by this change?

1st Senator   This cannot be,
By no assay of reason. 'Tis a pageant
To keep us in false gaze. When we consider
25   The importancy of Cyprus to the Turk,
And let ourselves again but understand
That as it more concerns the Turk than Rhodes,
So may he with more facile question bear it,
For that it stands not in such warlike brace,
30   But altogether lacks the abilities
That Rhodes is dressed in. If we make thought of this,
We must not think the Turk is so unskilful
To leave that latest which concerns him first,
Neglecting an attempt of ease and gain
35   To wake and wage a danger profitless.

Duke   Nay, in all confidence he's not for Rhodes.

1st Officer   Here is more news.

[*Enter a* **Messenger**]

Messenger   The Ottomites, reverend and gracious,
Steering with due course toward the isle of Rhodes,
40   Have there injointed with an after fleet.

1st Senator   Ay, so I thought. How many, as you guess?

1st Officer   A messenger from the galleys.

[*A* **Sailor** *enters*]

Duke   What's the latest?

Sailor   The Turkish fleet is making for Rhodes. Signor Angelo ordered me to report this to the Senate.

Duke   [*to the assembly*] How does this change of plan strike you?

1st Senator   It can't be true, by any stretch of the imagination. It's a bit of play-acting to distract our attention. When we consider the importance of Cyprus to the Turks, and remind ourselves that not only is Cyprus of more interest to the Turks than Rhodes, they can also capture it more easily, since it's not geared up for war, and altogether lacks the defences that Rhodes possesses. If we bear this in mind, we must not think the Turks are so incompetent that they would give their top priority second place, turning from easy pickings to provoke and fight a futile engagement.

Duke   Yes. They're not after Rhodes, we can be sure of that.

1st Officer   Here's more news.

[*A* **Messenger** *enters*]

Messenger   Your honours, the Ottomites, heading directly for Rhodes, have combined with a second fleet.

1st Senator   So I thought. How many, would you guess?

Messenger   Of thirty sail; and now they do re-stem
Their backward course, bearing with frank appearance
Their purposes toward Cyprus. Signor Montano,
45   Your trusty and most valiant servitor,
With his free duty recommends you thus,
And prays you to believe him.

Duke   'Tis certain then for Cyprus.
Marcus Luccicos is not here in town?

50   **1st Senator**   He's now at Florence.

Duke   Write from us: wish him
Post post-haste dispatch.

1st Senator   Here comes Brabantio and the valiant Moor.

[*Enter* **Brabantio, Othello, Iago, Roderigo** *and Officers*]

Duke   Valiant Othello, we must straight employ you
55   Against the general enemy Ottoman.
[*To* **Brabantio**] I did not see you. Welcome, gentle
    signor;
We lacked your counsel and your help tonight.

Brabantio   So did I yours. Good your grace, pardon me:
60   Neither my place, nor aught I heard of business,
Hath raised me from my bed; nor doth the general care
Take hold on me; for my particular grief
Is of so flood-gate and o'erbearing nature
That it engluts and swallows other sorrows
65   And yet is still itself.

Duke   Why, what's the matter?

Brabantio   My daughter! Oh, my daughter!

Senators   Dead?

Messenger Thirty ships. Now they've done a U-turn, making straight for Cyprus. Signor Montano, your loyal and most gallant Commander, with great respect informs you thus and trusts you will believe him.

Duke It's Cyprus for certain, then. Marcus Luccicos is in Venice, is he not?

1st Senator He's in Florence now.

Duke Send him a letter. Require his return, in double-quick time.

1st Senator Here come Brabantio and the valiant Moor.

[**Brabantio, Othello, Iago, Roderigo** *and Officers enter*]

Duke Valiant Othello, we must despatch you at once against our enemies the Turks. [*To* **Brabantio**] I didn't see you. Welcome, gentle signor; we lacked the benefit of your advice and help tonight.

Brabantio So did I yours. Your Grace, forgive me. Neither my being a Senator nor any news I heard, has got me out of bed. Nor are state matters on my mind. My personal grief is so overwhelming and all-consuming that it devours all other sorrows and still won't go away.

Duke Why? What's the matter?

Brabantio My daughter! Oh, my daughter!

Senators What, dead?

45

Brabantio   Ay, to me.
70   She is abused, stolen from me, and corrupted
      By spells and medicines bought of mountebanks;
      For nature so preposterously to err,
      Being not deficient, blind, or lame of sense,
      Sans witchcraft could not.

75 **Duke**   Who'er he be that in this foul proceeding
      Hath thus beguiled your daughter of herself
      And you of her, the bloody book of law
      You shall yourself read in the bitter letter
      After your own sense, yea, though our proper son
80   Stood in your action.

Brabantio   Humbly I thank your grace.
      Here is the man: this Moor, whom now it seems
      Your special mandate for the state affairs
      Hath hither brought.

85 **All**   We are very sorry for't.

Duke   (*to* **Othello**) What in your own part can you say to
      this?

Brabantio   Nothing, but this is so.

Othello   Most potent, grave and reverend signors,
90   My very noble and approved good masters.
      That I have ta'en away this old man's daughter,
      It is most true; true I have married her;
      The very head and front of my offending
      Hath this extent, no more. Rude am I in my speech
95   And little blessed with the soft phrase of peace;
      For since these arms of mine had seven years' pith
      Till now some nine moons wasted, they have used
      Their dearest action in the tented field;
      And little of this great world can I speak
100   More than pertains to feats of broil and battle;

Brabantio   Yes, as far as I'm concerned. She has been disgraced, stolen from me, and corrupted by spells and potions bought from disreputable doctors! Since she's neither sick, blind nor half-witted, she couldn't possibly have gone so wrong without the aid of witchcraft.

Duke   Whoever he may be in this foul business who has robbed your daughter of herself, and you of her, you shall be judge and jury in his trial and sentence him to death: yes, even if my own son were the guilty party.

Brabantio   I humbly thank your grace. [*Turning to* **Othello**] Here is the man: this Moor, the one it seems you have summoned here on state affairs.

All   How unfortunate –

Duke   [*To* **Othello**] What can you say in your own defence?

Brabantio   Nothing other than it's true!

Othello   All powerful, wise, and reverend signors; my most noble and respected masters. That I have taken away this old man's daughter is quite true. True I have married her. That is the top and bottom of my offence, no more. I am rough in my speech and little gifted with a silk tongue, for since I was seven till nine months ago these arms of mine have seen their greatest action on the battlefield. And I can speak little of this great world beyond what's related to feats of fighting and battle. So in

And therefore little shall I grace my cause
In speaking for myself. Yet, by your gracious patience,
I will a round unvarnished tale deliver
Of my whole course of love: what drugs, what charms,
105   What conjuration and what mighty magic –
For such proceedings I am charged withal –
I won his daughter.

Brabantio   A maiden never bold of spirit;
So still and quiet that her motion
110   Blushed at herself: and she, in spite of nature,
Of years, of country, credit, everything,
To fall in love with what she feared to look on!
It is a judgement maimed and most imperfect
That will confess perfection so could err
115   Against all rules of nature, and must be driven
To find out practices of cunning hell
Why this should be. I therefore vouch again
That with some mixtures powerful o'er the blood,
Or with some dram conjured to this effect,
120   He wrought upon her.

Duke   To vouch this is no proof,
Without more wider and more overt test
Than these thin habits and poor likelihoods
Of modern seeming do prefer against him.

125 **1st Senator**   But, Othello, speak:
Did you by indirect and forced courses
Subdue and poison this young maid's affections?
Or came it by request and such fair question
As soul to soul affordeth?

speaking on my own behalf I shall not enhance my cause. But with your gracious permission, I shall describe my whole love affair in plain blunt terms: the drugs, the charms, the spells and the mighty magic – for these are what I'm accused of – by which I won his daughter.

Brabantio   A modest maid, of such a still and quiet disposition that she blushed at her own shadow: and she – in spite of her natural duty, her youth, her country, her reputation, everything! – is supposed to have fallen in love with a man she was scared to look at! It would be flawed thinking to suppose that perfection could err like that, against all the rules of nature. Why it should happen can only be explained by identifying the fiendish practices at work. I therefore declare once more that with some powerful narcotics, or some drink made potent by spells, he manipulated her mind.

Duke   To declare this is not to prove it. There needs to be fuller and more obvious evidence than these simple arguments based on 'maybe' and 'perhaps'.

1st Senator   Othello, speak. Did you, by indirect and mind-affecting means, acquire control over, and poison, this young girl's affections? Or did you win her by courtship and such gentle talk as lovers exchange?

130 **Othello**   I do beseech you,
     Send for the lady to the Sagittary,
     And let her speak of me before her father.
     If you do find me foul in her report,
     The trust, the office I do hold of you
135 Not only take away, but let your sentence
     Even fall upon my life.

     Duke   Fetch Desdemona hither.

     Othello   Ancient, conduct them: you best know the place.

                              [*Exit* **Iago** *with Attendants*]

     And till she come, as truly as to heaven
140 I do confess the vices of my blood,
     So justly to your grave ears I'll present
     How I did thrive in this fair lady's love,
     And she in mine.

     Duke   Say it, Othello.

145 **Othello**   Her father loved me, oft invited me,
     Still questioned me the story of my life
     From year to year; the battles, sieges, fortunes
     That I have passed.
     I ran it through, even from my boyish days
150 To the very moment that he bade me tell it:
     Wherein I spake of most disastrous chances,
     Of moving accidents by flood and field,
     Of hair-breadth 'scapes in the imminent deadly breach,
     Of being taken by the insolent foe,
155 And sold to slavery; of my redemption thence,
     And portance in my travels' history:
     Wherein of antres vast and deserts idle,
     Rough quarries, rocks and hills whose heads touch
          heaven,
160 It was my hint to speak – such was the process:

Othello I beg you: send for the lady at the Arrow Inn, and let her speak of me in front of her father. If then you find me guilty, don't just strip me of the post and responsibility you have given me, but take my life as well.

Duke Fetch Desdemona here.

Othello [*To* **Iago**] Sergeant, show them the way. You know the place best.

[**Iago** *exits with Attendants*]

Till she comes, with the same honesty that I confess my sins to heaven, I'll tell you truthfully how I won this lady's love, and she mine.

Duke Tell us, Othello.

Othello Her father loved me; often invited me home; continually questioned me about the story of my life over the years – the battles, sieges, and adventures I have had. I recounted it, right from my boyhood to the very moment he asked me to tell it. In it I spoke of disastrous mishaps; of exciting incidents at sea and on land; of hair-breadth escapes in life-endangering breaches of enemy lines; of being captured by the cruel foe and sold to slavery; of gaining my liberty, and what happened afterwards. This, the way things went, was the occasion for me to tell about vast caves and empty deserts, deep quarries, rocks, and mountains whose peaks

And of the Cannibals that each other eat,
The Anthropophagi, and men whose heads
Do grow beneath their shoulders. This to hear
Would Desdemona seriously incline:
165 But still the house affairs would draw her thence,
Which ever as she could with haste dispatch
She'd come again, and with a greedy ear
Devour up my discourse; which I observing
Took once a pliant hour, and found good means
170 To draw from her a prayer of earnest heart
That I would all my pilgrimage dilate
Whereof by parcels she had something heard,
But not intentively. I did consent,
And often did beguile her of her tears
175 When I did speak of some distressful stroke
That my youth suffered. My story being done,
She gave me for my pains a world of sighs:
She swore, in faith 'twas strange, 'twas passing strange,
'Twas pitiful, 'twas wondrous pitiful;
180 She wished she had not heard it, yet she wished
That heaven had made her such a man. She thanked
     me,
And bade me, if I had a friend that loved her,
I should but teach him how to tell my story,
185 And that would woo her. Upon this hint I spake:
She loved me for the dangers I had passed,
And I loved her, that she did pity them.
This only is the witchcraft I have used.
Here comes the lady. Let her witness it.

[*Enter* **Desdemona, Iago,** *and Attendants*]

190 **Duke** I think this tale would win my daughter too.
Good Brabantio:
Take up this mangled matter at the best:
Men do their broken weapons rather use
Than their bare hands.

touched heaven; and of the cannibal tribes, and men whose heads were set in their chests. Desdemona was fascinated by this, but household duties would tear her away. She would finish them as quickly as possible and return, and greedily devour all I had to tell. Noticing this, I took a favourable opportunity on one occasion and was able to extract from her a heartfelt request for a full narration, of which she'd heard fragments but not the whole consecutive story. I agreed, and often drew her tears when I spoke of some distressing misfortune I'd suffered in my youth. My story told, she repaid me with innumerable sighs. She declared that 'Indeed, it was astonishing'; it was 'truly astonishing'; it was 'distressing'; 'terribly distressing'; she 'wished she hadn't heard it', yet she wished 'that God had made her such a man as that'. She thanked me, and asked me – if I had a friend who was fond of her – whether I would teach him how to tell my story, because that would win her heart. Given this hint, I spoke up. She loved me for the adventures I had had; and I loved her because she pitied them. This is the only witchcraft I have used. Here comes the lady: let her give her own evidence.

[**Desdemona** *enters, with* **Iago** *and Attendants*]

Duke I think this tale would win my daughter, too. Good Brabantio, make the best of a bad job. Better to use the stump of a sword than your bare hands.

195 **Brabantio**   I pray you hear her speak.
    If she confess that she was half the wooer,
    Destruction on me, if my bad blame
    Light on the man! Come hither, gentle mistress;
    Do you perceive in all this company
200 Where most you owe obedience?

    Desdemona   My noble father,
    I do perceive here a divided duty:
    To you I am bound for life and education;
    My life and education both do learn me
205 How to respect you. You are lord of all my duty,
    I am hitherto your daughter. But here's my husband;
    And so much duty as my mother showed
    To you, preferring you before her father,
    So much I challenge, that I may profess
210 Due to the Moor, my lord.

    Brabantio   God be wi'you! I have done.
    Please it your grace, on to the state affairs.
    I had rather to adopt a child than get it.
    Come hither, Moor:
215 I here do give thee that with all my heart
    Which, but thou hast already, with all my heart
    I would keep from thee. For your sake, jewel,
    I am glad at soul I have no other child,
    For thy escape would teach me tyranny
220 To hang clogs on them. I have done, my lord.

    Duke   Let me speak like yourself and lay a sentence
    Which, as a grise or step, may help these lovers
    Into your favour.
    When remedies are past, the griefs are ended
225 By seeing the worst, which late on hopes depended.
    To mourn a mischief that is past and gone
    Is the next way to draw new mischief on.

Brabantio Let her speak. If she confesses she did half the wooing, bad luck to me if I blame the man! Come here, young lady. Where in all this company do you most owe obedience?

Desdemona My noble father, that implies a divided loyalty. To you I am indebted for my life and upbringing. My life and upbringing teach me how to respect you. You have all the duty that I owe you as your daughter. But here is my husband. And such duty as my mother gave to you – putting you before her father – so much I lay claim to, as belonging to the Moor, my lord.

Brabantio God's blessing on you. I'll say no more. [*To the* **Duke**] If it so please your Grace, turn now to state affairs. Better to adopt a child than father one. [*Taking* **Desdemona's** *hand, and addressing* **Othello**] Come here, Moor. I hereby give you, with all my heart, what you already have and what – with all my heart – I would wish to keep from you. [*He passes* **Desdemona** *over to* **Othello**] Because of you, jewel, I am heartily glad I have no other child. Your elopement would make a tyrant of me: I'd make her wear a ball and chain. I have no more to say, my lord.

Duke Let me speak for you instead, and quote some proverbs which might help to bring these lovers into your favour. 'When things can't be cured, all grieving is ended; the worst is endured when all hope's suspended'. 'To mourn a trouble past and gone will only make another one'. 'Whatever be

What cannot be preserved when fortune takes,
Patience her injury a mockery makes.
230 The robbed that smiles steals something from the thief;
He robs himself that spends a bootless grief.

Brabantio   So let the Turk of Cyprus us beguile,
We lose it not so long as we can smile.
He bears the sentence well that nothing bears
235 But the free comfort which from thence he hears;
But he bears both the sentence and the sorrow
That, to pay grief, must of poor patience borrow.
These sentences, to sugar or to gall,
Being strong on both sides, are equivocal.
240 But words are words; I never yet did hear
That the bruised heart was pierced through the ear.
Beseech you now, to the affairs of state.

Duke   The Turk with a most mighty preparation makes
for Cyprus. Othello, the fortitude of the place is best
245 known to you: and though we have there a substitute of
most allowed sufficiency, yet opinion, sovereign mistress
of effects, throws a more safer voice on you. You must
therefore be content to slubber the gloss of your new
fortunes with this more stubborn and boisterous
250 expedition.

Othello   The tyrant custom, most grave Senators,
Hath made the flinty and steel couch of war
My thrice-driven bed of down. I do agnize
A natural and prompt alacrity
255 I find in hardness; and do undertake
This present war against the Ottomites.
Most humbly, therefore, bending to your state,
I crave fit disposition for my wife,
Due reference of place and exhibition,
260 With such accommodation and besort
As levels with her breeding.

misfortune's pain, Patience will make well again.'
'The robbed who smiles steals something from the
thief. He robs himself who wastes his time in grief.'

Brabantio [*replying in the same idiom but ironically*]
So 'let the Turks steal Cyprus, our fair isle; we've
lost it not so long as we can smile . . .' 'He little
suffers who is forced to hear smooth platitudes that
soothe the ear. But he who's given glib advice and
counselled to be patient, suffers twice.' 'These
proverbs which can soothe or sting, two meanings
to the issue bring. But words are words; I never yet
did hear that broken hearts were mended through
the ear.' [*He calls a halt to this exchange of wit*]
With the greatest respect: proceed to the affairs of
state.

Duke The Turks are making for Cyprus with a huge
fleet. Othello, you best know the strength of the
place, and though we have a very sound viceroy
there, public opinion (the final arbiter) has more
confidence in you. You must therefore be willing to
have the shine taken off your new fortunes by this
tough and dangerous expedition.

Othello Habit, distinguished Senators, has made the
harsh discomforts of war a bed of swansdown for
me. I admit that I find hardship attractive. I'll fight
this war against the Turks. Humbly, therefore, and
with respect, I request appropriate arrangements be
made for my wife: treatment which accords with
her rank; adequate maintenance; and such
accommodation and servants as is in keeping with
her breeding.

Duke   If you please,
Be't at her father's.

Brabantio   I'll not have it so.

265 **Othello**   Nor I.

Desdemona   Nor I: I would not there reside
To put my father in impatient thoughts
By being in his eye. Most gracious Duke,
To my unfolding lend a gracious ear,
270   And let me find a charter in your voice
To assist my simpleness.

Duke   What would you, Desdemona?

Desdemona   That I did love the Moor to live with him,
My downright violence and storm of fortunes
275   May trumpet to the world. My heart's subdued
Even to the very quality of my lord.
I saw Othello's visage in his mind
And to his honours and his valiant parts
Did I my soul and fortunes consecrate.
280   So that, dear lords, if I be left behind
A moth of peace, and he go to the war,
The rites for which I love him are bereft me,
And I a heavy interim shall support
By his dear absence. Let me go with him.

285 **Othello**   Your voices, Lords: beseech you, let her will
Have a free way. I therefore beg it not
To please the palate of my appetite,
Nor to comply with heat – the young affects
In me defunct – and proper satisfaction;
290   But to be free and bounteous to her mind:
And heaven defend your good souls that you think
I will your serious and great business scant
For she is with me. No, when light-winged toys

Duke   If it's acceptable to you, let her stay at her
  father's.

Brabantio   I don't agree.

Othello   Nor I.

Desdemona   Nor I. I wouldn't live there to irritate my
  father by being in his sight. Most gracious Duke,
  consider my proposal favourably; and may you
  return a soft answer to help me in my simplicity.

Duke   What is your wish? Speak.

Desdemona   That I love the Moor and wish to live
  with him, my extremely stormy fortunes proclaim to
  all the world. My love is at his service, to the
  utmost. Let me go with him.

Othello   Give her your consent. Let her have her way.
  Heaven knows I do not ask to satisfy my appetite,
  nor out of carnal need − I am no young lover! − but
  to enjoy her intellectual company. Heaven forbid
  that you should think I will neglect your highly
  important affairs because she is with me. No, if ever

Of feathered Cupid seel with wanton dullness
295 My speculative and officed instruments,
That my disports corrupt and taint my business,
Let housewives make a skillet of my helm,
And all indign and base adversities
Make head against my reputation!

300 **Duke** Be it as you shall privately determine,
Either for her stay, or going. The affair cries haste,
And speed must answer. You must away tonight.

Desdemona Tonight, my lord?

Duke   This night.

305 **Othello**   With all my heart.

Duke At nine i'the morning, here we'll meet again.
Othello, leave some officer behind,
And he shall our commission bring to you,
With such things else of quality and respect
310 As doth import you.

Othello   So please your grace, my Ancient,
A man he is of honesty and trust:
To his conveyance I assign my wife,
With what else needful your good grace shall think
315 To be sent after me.

Duke   Let it be so.
Good night to everyone. And noble signor,
If virtue no delighted beauty lack,
Your son-in-law is far more fair than black.

320 **1st Senator** Adieu, brave Moor; use Desdemona well.

Brabantio Look to her, Moor, if thou hast eyes to see.
She has deceived her father, and may thee.

[*Exeunt* **Duke, Senators,** *and Attendants*]

I am so blinded and befuddled by Cupid's darts,
that my amorous pleasures conflict with business,
let housewives make a saucepan of my helmet, and
shameful scandal ruin my reputation!

Duke   Do as you shall decide between you, either for
her to go or to stay. This incident demands a quick
response. You must leave tonight.

Desdemona   Tonight, my lord?

Duke   This very night.

Othello   With all my heart.

Duke   At nine tomorrow morning, we'll meet here
again. Othello, leave an officer behind, and he'll
bring our commission to you, with various
confidential documents of concern to you.

Othello   If it so please your Grace, I'll leave my Staff-
Sergeant. He is a man of honesty and trust. I'll leave
him to look after my wife, and any other matters
which your Grace thinks ought to be sent after me.

Duke   By all means. Goodnight to everyone. [*To*
Brabantio] Noble signor, if valour is the measure of
true beauty, your son is fairer than he's black!

1st Senator   Adieu, brave Moor. Be good to
Desdemona.

Brabantio   Keep your eye on her, Moor, unless you
are blind. She has deceived her father, and might
deceive you.

[*The* **Duke, Senators** *and Attendants leave*]

Othello   My life upon her faith! Honest Iago,
My Desdemona must I leave to thee.
325 I prithee let thy wife attend on her,
And bring them after in the best advantage.
Come, Desdemona, I have but an hour
Of love, of worldly matters and direction
To spend with thee. We must obey the time.

[*Exeunt* **Othello** *and* **Desdemona**]

330 **Roderigo**   Iago –

Iago   What say'st thou, noble heart?

Roderigo   What will I do, thinkest thou?

Iago   Why, go to bed and sleep.

Roderigo   I will incontinently drown myself.

335 **Iago**   If thou dost, I shall never love thee after. Why, thou
silly gentleman!

Roderigo   It is silliness to live, when to live is torment; and
then we have a prescription to die, when death is our
physician.

340 **Iago**   Oh villainous! I have looked upon the world for four
times seven years, and since I could distinguish betwixt a
benefit and an injury, I never found a man that knew
how to love himself. Ere I would say I would drown
myself for the love of a guinea-hen, I would change my
345 humanity with a baboon.

Roderigo   What should I do? I confess it is my shame to
be so fond, but it is not in my virtue to amend it.

Othello   I'd wager my life upon her faithfulness!

Honest Iago, I must leave my Desdemona with you.
Let your wife look after her, and have them follow
me at the most convenient opportunity. Come,
Desdemona: I have only one hour of love, of
business matters and instructions to spend with
you. We mustn't waste time.

[**Othello** *and* **Desdemona** *leave*]

Roderigo   Iago –

Iago   What's on your mind, noble heart?

Roderigo   What do you think I should do?

Iago   Why, go to bed and sleep.

Roderigo   I'll drown myself right now!

Iago   If you do, I'll never speak to you again. Why,
you silly man!

Roderigo   Is it silly to live, when life is a torment?
When death is our doctor, we have his prescription
to die.

Iago   Outrageous! I'm twenty-eight years old, and
ever since I could distinguish between a benefit and
an injury, I've never found a man who knew how to
love himself. Before I'd say I'd drown myself for the
love of a bit of skirt, I'd change places with a
baboon.

Roderigo   What should I do? I know it's ridiculous to
be so much in love, but I can't stop myself.

Iago Virtue? A fig! 'Tis in ourselves that we are thus, or
thus. Our bodies are our gardens, to the which our wills
350   are gardeners. So that if we will plant nettles or sow
lettuce, set hyssop and weed up thyme, supply it with
one gender of herbs or distract it with many, either to
have it sterile with idleness or manured with industry,
why, the power and corrigible authority of this lies in our
355   wills. If the balance of our lives had not one scale of
reason to poise another of sensuality, the blood and
baseness of our natures would conduct us to most
preposterous conclusions. But we have reason to cool our
raging motions, our carnal stings, our unbitted lusts:
360   whereof I take this, that you call love, to be a sect or
scion.

Roderigo It cannot be.

Iago It is merely a lust of the blood and a permission of
the will. Come, be a man. Drown thyself? Drown cats
365   and blind puppies. I have professed me thy friend, and I
confess me knit to thy deserving with cables of
perdurable toughness. I could never better stead thee
than now. Put money in thy purse. Follow thou these
wars; defeat thy favour with an usurped beard. I say,
370   put money in thy purse. It cannot be that Desdemona
should long continue her love to the Moor – put money
in thy purse – nor he to her. It was a violent
commencement, and thou shalt see an answerable
sequestration; put but money in thy purse. These Moors
375   are changeable in their wills: fill thy purse with money.
The food that to him now is as luscious as locusts shall
be to him shortly as bitter as the coloquintida. When she
is sated with his body she will find the error of her
choice. She must have change, she must. Therefore put

Iago   Can't? Nonsense! It's up to us whether we are
this, or that. Our bodies are our gardens, and our
willpower acts as the gardeners. So if we plant
nettles or sow lettuce; put in scented herb and
weed out thyme; stock it with one strain of herbs or
many different ones; either have it unproductive
through idleness or cultivated by hard work; why,
the controlling power in these matters lies in our
wills. If we didn't have two scales in our lives, one
balanced against the other – reason in one and
sensuality in the other – the passionate and lusty
part of our natures would make us do the most
ridiculous things. But we have common sense to
cool our ardour, our physical impulses, our
unbridled lusts. What you call 'love', it seems to me,
is only an offshoot of this.

Roderigo   Surely not?

Iago   It's just your lust, which your willpower has
permitted. Come on: be a man! Drown yourself?
Drown cats and blind puppies! I have befriended
you, and I am bound to your cause with chains of
everlasting strength. I could never do you more
good than now. Make yourself some money! Enlist
in the war. Disguise your face with a beard. I tell
you – make yourself some money! Desdemona
can't possibly love her Moor for very long – make
yourself some money – and he'll tire of her. It had a
passionate beginning, and you'll see it will have a
corresponding kind of end. Just make yourself
some money! These Moors are temperamental. Get
rich! The food that right now is as luscious as
strawberries will soon be as bitter as crab apples.
When she's had enough of his body, she'll find
she's made a big mistake. She must have change,

65

380   money in thy purse. If thou wilt needs damn thyself, do
it a more delicate way than drowning. Make all the
money thou canst. If sanctimony and a frail vow betwixt
an erring barbarian and a super-subtle Venetian be not
too hard for my wits and all the tribe of hell, thou shalt
385   enjoy her. Therefore make money. A pox of drowning
thyself! It is clean out of the way. Seek thou rather to be
hanged in compassing thy joy than to be drowned and
go without her.

Roderigo   Wilt thou be fast to my hopes, if I depend on
390   the issue?

Iago   Thou art sure of me. Go, make money. I have told
thee often, and I tell thee again and again, I hate the
Moor. My cause is hearted: thine hath no less reason.
Let us be conjunctive in our revenge against him. If thou
395   canst cuckold him, thou dost thyself a pleasure, me a
sport. There are many events in the womb of time,
which will be delivered. Traverse! Go, provide thy
money. We will have more of this tomorrow. Adieu.

Roderigo   Where shall we meet in the morning?

400 **Iago**   At my lodging.

Roderigo   I'll be with thee betimes.

Iago   Go to; farewell. Do you hear, Roderigo?

Roderigo   What say you?

Iago   No more of drowning, do you hear?

405 **Roderigo**   I am changed.

Iago   Go to; farewell! Put money enough in your purse.

Roderigo   I'll go sell all my land.

[*Exit*]

she must. Therefore: put money in your pocket. If you are determined to be damned, do it some better way than by drowning. Make all the money you can. If holiness and a mere marriage-vow between a tom-cat of a barbarian and an impressionable Venetian girl don't prove too hard for my wits and all the devils in hell, you'll have her. Therefore: raise some money. Sod drowning yourself! It's out of the question. You might as well be hanged for laying her as be drowned and never have her.

Roderigo   Will you be loyal to me if I trust you?

Iago   You can be sure of me. Go and make some money. I've told you often enough and I'll tell you again and again: I hate the Moor. My cause is heartfelt. Yours has no less justification. Let us work together in our revenge against him. If you can have her on the side, you'll do yourself a favour and give me some fun. Time has surprises in store. Go – get your money. We'll talk more about this tomorrow. Adieu!

Roderigo   Where shall we meet in the morning?

Iago   At my lodgings.

Roderigo   I'll be there early.

Iago   Sure. Farewell. Now listen, Roderigo –

Roderigo   Yes!

Iago   No more of this drowning, do you hear?

Roderigo   I'm converted.

Iago   Good. Farewell! Fill your pockets with money!

Roderigo   I'll sell all my land.

[*He goes*]   67

Iago   Thus do I ever make my fool my purse:
For I mine own gained knowledge should profane
410   If I would time expend with such a snipe
But for my sport and profit. I hate the Moor,
And it is thought abroad that 'twixt my sheets
He's done my office. I know not if't be true
But I, for mere suspicion in that kind,
415   Will do as if for surety. He holds me well:
The better shall my purpose work on him.
Cassio's a proper man; let me see now;
To get his place and to plume up my will
In double knavery – How? How? Let me see.
420   After some time, to abuse Othello's ear
That he is too familiar with his wife.
He has a person and a smooth dispose
To be suspected – framed to make women false.
The Moor is of a free and open nature,
425   That thinks men honest that but seem to be so,
And will as tenderly be led by the nose –
As asses are.
I have't. It is engendered. Hell and night.
Must bring this monstrous birth to the world's light.

[*Exit*]

Iago   That's how I always get money from fools. It would be an insult to my intelligence if I wasted time on such a thickhead, if it wasn't for the sport and the profit. I hate the Moor, and it is generally thought that he has slept with my wife. I don't know whether that's true, but mere suspicion is good enough to set me off. He thinks well of me: that'll make my task easier. Cassio's a respectable man – Let me see now – How can I contrive to get his job and, making double mischief, do myself some good? How? How? Let me see – After a suitable period of time – to hint to Othello that Cassio spends too much time with his wife – He has the personality and the easy manner that lends itself to suspicion; just the thing for seducing women. The Moor has a generous and open nature, and thinks men trustworthy who only seem to be so. He'll be led by the nose. That's it! The plan's conceived. Evil must effect its monstrous birth!

[*He goes*]

Act two

Scene 1

A seaport in Cyprus. Enter **Montano** *and two* **Gentlemen.**

Montano   What from the cape can you discern at sea?

1st Gentleman   Nothing at all; it is a high-wrought flood.
I cannot 'twixt the heaven and the main
Descry a sail.

5 **Montano**   Methinks the wind does speak aloud at land;
A fuller blast ne'er shook our battlements.
If it hath ruffianed so upon the sea,
What ribs of oak, when the huge mountains melt on
them,
10 Can hold the mortise? What shall we hear of this?

2nd Gentleman   A segregation of the Turkish fleet:
For do but stand upon the foaming shore,
The chidden billow seems to pelt the clouds;
The wind-shaked surge, with high and monstrous mane,
15 Seems to cast water on the burning Bear
And quench the guards of the ever-fixed Pole.
I never did like molestation view
On the enchafed flood.

Montano   If that the Turkish fleet
20 Be not ensheltered and embayed, they are drowned:
It is impossible they bear it out.

Act two

Scene 1

*The harbour at Cyprus. The Governor, **Montano**, enters with two gentlemen.*

Montano [*looking out to sea*] What can you see from the cape?

1st Gentleman Nothing at all. It's extremely stormy. I cannot detect a sail between the sky and the sea.

Montano The wind is roaring on land: nothing fiercer has ever shaken our battlements. If it has raged like this at sea, what ships could hold together when huge mountainous waves descend upon them? What will come of this?

2nd Gentleman The Turkish fleet will be scattered. You have only to stand on the foaming shore: the lashing waves seem to pelt the clouds. The windswept ocean, with its high and monster-like white manes, appears to drench the fiery Little Bear, and quench the stars that guard the never-moving Pole. I've never seen a storm at sea to equal it.

Montano If the Turkish fleet hasn't taken refuge in harbour, they'll all be drowned. They couldn't possibly sit this out.

[*Enter* **3rd Gentleman**]

3rd Gentleman   News, Lords! Our wars are done:
The desperate tempest hath so banged the Turks
That their designment halts. A noble ship of Venice
25   Hath seen a grievous wrack and sufferance
On most part of their fleet.

Montano   How; is this true?

3rd Gentleman   The ship is here put in;
A Veronesa, Michael Cassio,
30   Lieutenant to the warlike Moor, Othello,
Is come ashore: the Moor himself at sea,
And is in full commission here for Cyprus.

Montano   I am glad on't; 'tis a worthy governor.

3rd Gentleman   But this same Cassio, though he speak of
35   comfort
Touching the Turkish loss, yet he looks sadly
And prays the Moor be safe; for they were parted
With foul and violent tempest.

Montano   Pray heaven he be:
40   For I have served him, and the man commands
Like a full soldier. Let's to the seaside, ho!
As well to see the vessel that's come in,
As to throw out our eyes for brave Othello,
Even till we make the main and the aerial blue
45   An indistinct regard.

3rd Gentleman   Come, let's do so,
For every minute is expectancy
Of more arrivance.

[A **Gentleman** *enters*]

3rd Gentleman   News, Lords! The war is over! The awesome tempest has battered the Turks so much their plan is sabotaged. A noble Venetian ship has witnessed the destruction of most of their fleet.

Montano   What: is this true?

3rd Gentleman   The ship is here in port: a cutter. Michael Cassio, lieutenant to the Moor Othello, has come ashore. The Moor himself is at sea, and making straight for Cyprus.

Montano   I'm very glad to hear it. He's a good commander.

3rd Gentleman   This Cassio, though he's brought good news about the Turkish losses, is worried nonetheless. He prays the Moor is safe. They were separated by the foul and violent tempest.

Montano   Pray God he is. I've served under him, and he commands like a real soldier. Let's go down to the waterfront to see the ship that's just arrived and to keep a look-out for the brave Othello till we can't tell sea from sky.

3rd Gentleman   Let's do that. We expect more ships to arrive every minute.

[*Enter* **Cassio**]

Cassio   Thanks, you the valiant of this warlike isle
50   That so approve the Moor, and let the heavens
Give him defence against the elements,
For I have lost him on a dangerous sea.

Montano   Is he well shipped?

Cassio   His bark is stoutly timbered, and his pilot
55   Of very expert and approved allowance;
Therefore my hopes, not surfeited to death,
Stand in bold cure.

[*A cry within 'A sail, a sail, a sail!' Enter a* **Messenger**]

Cassio   What noise?

Messenger   The town is empty; on the brow o'the sea
60   Stand ranks of people, and they cry 'A sail!'

Cassio   My hopes do shape him for the Governor.

[*A shot*]

2nd Gentleman   They do discharge their shot of courtesy:
Our friends at least.

Cassio   I pray you, sir, go forth,
65   And give us truth who 'tis that is arrived.

2nd Gentleman   I shall.

[*Exit*]

Montano   But, good Lieutenant, is your General wived?

Cassio   Most fortunately; he hath achieved a maid
That paragons description and wild fame;
70   One that excels the quirks of blazoning pens,
And in the essential vesture of creation
Does bear all excellency.

[**Cassio** *enters*]

Cassio   Thanks, soldiers of this fortified island, who
support the Moor! May God defend him against the
elements! I've lost contact with him on a dangerous
sea.

Montano   Is his ship in good condition?

Cassio   It's stoutly timbered, and his pilot is highly
regarded amongst the experts. I'm reasonably
confident.

[*Cries are heard: 'A ship! A ship! A ship!'*]

Cassio   What's that?

Messenger   The town is empty. Crowds are standing
on the seashore shouting 'A ship! A ship!'

Cassio   I hope it is the Commander.

[*A shot is fired*]

2nd Gentleman   They've fired their courtesy shot.
They are friendly, anyway.

Cassio   Go ahead if you will, sir, and tell us exactly
who has arrived.

2nd Gentleman   I shall.

[*He goes*]

Montano   Tell me, good Lieutenant: has your General
married?

Cassio   Most advantageously. He has won a maiden
who surpasses her description and renown. The
most gifted pens could not find adequate words;
her natural beauty is incomparable.

[*Enter* **2nd Gentleman**]

How now? Who has put in?

2nd Gentleman   'Tis one Iago, Ancient to the General.

75 **Cassio**   He's had most favourable and happy speed:
Tempests themselves, high seas, and howling winds,
The guttered rocks and congregated sands,
Traitors ensteeped to clog the guiltless keel,
As having sense of beauty, do omit
80 Their common natures, letting go safely by
The divine Desdemona

Montano   What is she?

Cassio   She that I spoke of, our great Captain's Captain,
Left in the conduct of the bold Iago;
85 Whose footing here anticipates our thoughts
A se'nnight's speed. Great Jove, Othello guard,
And swell his sail with thine own powerful breath,
That he may bless this bay with his tall ship,
And swiftly come to Desdemona's arms;
90 Give renewed fire to our extincted spirits,
And bring all Cyprus comfort!

[*Enter* **Desdemona, Emilia, Iago, Roderigo,** *and*
Attendants]

                                        Oh, behold,
The riches of the ship is come ashore!
Ye men of Cyprus, let her have your knees:
95 Hail to thee, lady! And the grace of heaven,
Before, behind thee, and on every hand,
Enwheel thee round!

Desdemona   I thank you, valiant Cassio.
What tidings can you tell me of my lord?

[*The* **2nd Gentleman** *enters*]

Well? Who has arrived?

2nd Gentleman   A man called Iago, the General's
Staff-Sergeant.

Cassio   He's done well to get here so quickly.
Tempests, high seas and howling winds, jagged
rocks and sandbanks – traitors lurking under water
to grind ships to a halt – out of respect for beauty
act out of character, letting the divine Desdemona
go safely by.

Montano   Who is she?

Cassio   The one I spoke about: our great Captain's
wife, left in the safe keeping of the bold Iago, whose
landing here is a week earlier than we expected.
Jove, guard Othello. Fill his sails with your own
powerful winds, so he may grace this harbour with
his tall ship; swiftly come to Desdemona's arms;
rekindle our morale; and bring all Cyprus comfort!

[**Desdemona, Emilia (Iago's** *wife*), **Iago, Roderigo**
and Attendants enter.]

Oh look! The ship's treasure has come on shore!
[*To the crowd*] men of Cyprus, on your knees! [*To*
Desdemona] Greetings, lady! And may the grace of
heaven encompass you!

Desdemona   Thank you, valiant Cassio. What news
have you of my husband?

100 **Cassio** He is not yet arrived; nor know I aught
But that he's well, and will be shortly here.

Desdemona Oh, but I fear! How lost you company?

Cassio The great contention of the sea and skies
Parted our fellowship.

[*Within: 'A sail, a sail!'*]

105   But hark, a sail!

[*A shot*]

2nd Gentleman They give their greeting to the citadel:
This likewise is a friend.

Cassio   See for the news.

[*Exit* **Gentleman**]

Good Ancient, you are welcome. Welcome, mistress.
110 Let it not gall your patience, good Iago,
That I extend my manners; 'tis my breeding
That gives me this bold show of courtesy.

[*He kisses* **Emilia**]

Iago Sir, would she give you so much of her lips
As of her tongue she oft bestows on me,
115 You'd have enough.

Desdemona Alas, she has no speech.

Iago   In faith, too much.
I find it still when I have list to sleep.
Marry, before your ladyship, I grant
120 She puts her tongue a little in her heart
And chides with thinking.

Emilia   You have little cause to say so.

Cassio   He has not yet arrived. I know no more than that he's well, and will be here soon.

Desdemona   That worries me! How did you lose contact with him?

Cassio   We were parted by the storm.

[*A cry is heard: 'A ship! A ship!'*]
Listen! A ship!

3rd Gentleman   They've fired their shot. This is also friendly.

Cassio   See what the news is. [*The* **Gentleman** *leaves. To* **Iago**] Sergeant, you are welcome. [*To* **Emilia**] Welcome, madam. Don't be vexed, good Iago, if I go further. This liberty is natural to my upbringing.

[*He kisses her*]

Iago   Sir, if she gave you as much of her lips as she often gives me of her tongue, you'd be more than satisfied.

Desdemona   Alas, she says very little.

Iago   Too much, believe me! It stops when I have permission to sleep. Though when she's with your ladyship, I admit she holds her tongue and keeps her shrewish thoughts to herself.

Emilia   You've no grounds for saying that!

Iago   Come on, come on: you are pictures out of doors,
    bells in your parlours, wild-cats in your kitchens, saints
125 in your injuries, devils being offended, players in your
    housewifery, and housewives in your beds.

Desdemona   Oh, fie upon thee, slanderer!

Iago   Nay, it is true, or else I am a Turk;
    You rise to play and go to bed to work.

130 **Emilia**   You shall not write my praise.

Iago   No, let me not.

Desdemona   What wouldst thou write of me, if thou
    shouldst praise me?

Iago   Oh, gentle lady, do not put me to't,
135 For I am nothing if not critical.

Desdemona   Come on, assay. There's one gone to the
    harbour?

Iago   Ay, madam.

Desdemona   I am not merry, but I do beguile
140 The thing I am by seeming otherwise.
    Come, how wouldst thou praise me?

Iago   I am about it, but indeed my invention
    Comes from my pate as birdlime does from frieze –
    It plucks out brains and all. But my muse labours,
145 And thus she is delivered:
    If she be fair and wise, fairness and wit,
    The one's for use, the other useth it.

Desdemona   Well praised! How if she be black and witty?

Iago   If she be black, and thereto have a wit,
150 She'll find a white that shall her blackness fit.

Iago   Come on, come on: you are mute out of doors;
chatterboxes in your own sitting rooms; wild-cats in
your kitchens; saints in inflicting hurts; devils when
you're the victims; play-actors when you keep
house; and real madams in your beds.

Desdemona   Really! You slanderer!

Iago   No, it's true, or I'm a villain. You get up to play,
and go to bed to work.

Emilia   You'll not write my reference!

Iago   Heaven forbid!

Desdemona   What would you say of me, if you were
writing a testimonial?

Iago   Oh, gentle lady, do not push me: I am nothing if
not critical.

Desdemona   Come on: try! Someone's gone to the
harbour?

Iago   Yes, madam.

Desdemona   [*aside*] I am not happy. I hide my real
feelings by seeming otherwise. [*To* **Iago**] Come on,
how would you describe me?

Iago   I'm thinking about it, but my mind gives forth
inspiration like glue comes off fabric: it's coming
out brains and all. But my Muse toils hard, and this
is what she comes up with:
If she's pretty and clever, with fair looks and brains,
The first is for use, while the second's for gains . . .

Desdemona   Apt! But what if she's black and clever?

Iago   If she is black, and with it is smart
She'll find a white man who's her counterpart . . .

Desdemona   Worse and worse.

Emilia   How if fair and foolish?

Iago   She never yet was foolish that was fair,
For even her folly helped her to an heir.

155 **Desdemona**   These are old fond paradoxes to make fools
laugh i'the alehouse. What miserable praise hast thou for
her that's foul and foolish?

Iago   There's none so foul and foolish thereunto,
But does foul pranks which fair and wise ones do.

160 **Desdemona**   Oh heavy ignorance! Thou praisest the worst
best! But what praise couldst thou bestow on a deserving
woman indeed? One that in the authority of her merit did
justly put on the vouch of very malice itself?

Iago   She that was ever fair and never proud,
165   Had tongue at will, and yet was never loud;
Never lacked gold, and yet went never gay;
Fled from her wish, and yet said 'Now I may';
She that, being angered, her revenge being nigh,
Bade her wrong stay, and her displeasure fly;
170   She that in wisdom never was so frail
To change the cod's head for the salmon's tail;
She that could think and ne'er disclose her mind:
See suitors following and not look behind;
She was a wight, if ever such wight were –

175 **Desdemona**   To do what?

Iago   To suckle fools, and chronicle small beer.

Desdemona   Oh, most lame and impotent conclusion! Do
not learn of him, Emilia, though he be thy husband.
How say you, Cassio. Is he not a most profane and
180   liberal counsellor?

Desdemona   Worse and worse!

Emilia   What if pretty and foolish?

Iago   She never yet was foolish that was fair.
For even her folly helped her: to an heir . . .

Desdemona   These are silly old sayings to make
idiots laugh over a pint. What cynical remarks have
you got for the woman who's ugly and foolish?

Iago   No woman's so ugly and foolish too
That she doesn't sin like the nice ones do . . .

Desdemona   Oh, such ignorance! You praise the
worst most. But what praise could you give to a
worthy woman indeed? One who's so good that
even malice itself would rightly praise her?

Iago   She that was always nice and never proud;
Spoke when she should, and yet was never loud;
Never lacked cash, but never flaunted dress;
Repressed her desires. but knew when to say 'yes';
She who, aggrieved, and with vengeance at hand
Suffered the wrong, and let temper disband;
She whose behaviour was never so stupid
That bad became worse, dictated by Cupid;
She who could think, but not speak her mind;
See suitors pursue, and not look behind;
She was a wench, if such a wench was ever –

Desdemona   To do what?

Iago   To suckle babes and talk about the weather!

Desdemona   What a weak and feeble conclusion!
Don't take any notice of him, Emilia, even though
he is your husband. What do you think, Cassio?
Isn't he a very vulgar and bawdy tutor?

Cassio   He speaks home, madam; you may relish him
more in the soldier than in the scholar.

Iago   (*aside*) He takes her by the palm. Ay, well said,
whisper. As little a web as this will ensnare as great a
185   fly as Cassio. Ay, smile upon her, do. I will catch you in
your own courtesies. You say true, 'tis so indeed. If such
tricks as these strip you out of your lieutenantry, it had
been better you had not kissed your three fingers so oft,
which now again you are most apt to play the sir in.
190   Good: well kissed, an excellent courtesy! 'Tis so indeed.
Yet again, your fingers to your lips? Would they were
clyster-pipes for your sake!

[*Trumpets within*]

The Moor! I know his trumpet.

Cassio   'Tis truly so.

195 **Desdemona**   Let's meet him and receive him.

Cassio   Lo, where he comes!

[*Enter* **Othello** *and* **Attendants**]

Othello   Oh, my fair warrior!

Desdemona   My dear Othello!

Cassio   He doesn't mince his words, madam. He's best judged as a soldier rather than a scholar.

[*He walks to one side with* **Desdemona** *and they talk together*]

Iago   [*aside*] He takes her by the hand. Oh yes, well said; go on, whisper! With no bigger web than this I'll catch no less a fly than Cassio. Yes, smile at her, do. I'll tie you in knots with this flirting of yours! (*Catching their eye, he smiles genially and waves*] How right you are! Very true! [*Back to himself again*] If these little pleasantries lose you your lieutenantship, you'll regret your habit of throwing so many gallant kisses at the ladies. [*As he speaks,* **Cassio** *again kisses his fingers in a gesture of polite gallantry*] Very good! Well kissed! Very courteous! [*Smiling and nodding to them affably*] Yes, of course! [*Resuming his natural manner*] Your fingers to your lips yet again? Would they were roving elsewhere, for your sake!

[*A trumpet sounds*]

[*aloud*] The Moor! I recognize his trumpet!

Cassio   Indeed you are right.

Desdemona   Let's go meet him and give him welcome!

Cassio   Look, here he is!

[**Othello** *enters with Attendants*]

Othello   [*to* **Desdemona**] My lovely warrior!

Desdemona   [*embracing him*] My dear Othello!

Othello   It gives me wonder great as my content,
200   To see you here before me. Oh, my soul's joy!
       If after every tempest come such calms,
       May the winds blow till they have wakened death,
       And let the labouring bark climb hills of seas,
       Olympus-high, and duck again as low
205   As hell's from heaven! If it were now to die,
       'Twere now to be most happy; for I fear
       My soul hath her content so absolute
       That not another comfort like to this
       Succeeds in unknown fate.

210 **Desdemona**   The heavens forbid
       But that our loves and comforts should increase,
       Even as our days do grow.

     Othello   Amen to that, sweet Powers!
       I cannot speak enough of this content;
215   It stops me here; it is too much of joy.
       And this, and this the greatest discords be

     [*They kiss*]

     That e'er our hearts shall make.

     Iago   [*aside*] Oh, you are well tuned now!
       But I'll set down the pegs that make this music,
220   As honest as I am.

     Othello   Come, let's to the castle.
       News, friend. Our wars are done; the Turks are
          drowned.
       How do our old acquaintance of the isle?
225   Honey, you shall be well desired in Cyprus:
       I have found great love amongst them. Oh my sweet,
       I prattle out of fashion and I dote
       In mine own comforts. I prithee, good Iago

Othello   To see you here before me is as wonderful
as it is pleasant. Oh, my source of all happiness! If
calms like this could follow every storm, may the
winds blow till they awake the dead; let struggling
ships climb mountainous seas, and plunge down
again as far as hell is from heaven! This would be a
fitting time to die. My happiness is so complete I'll
never equal it.

Desdemona   Let us hope our love and happiness will
increase as we grow older!

Othello   Amen to that, oh Lord! My joy is beyond
words; I'm too overwhelmed to speak. [*He kisses
her*] May this [*he kisses her again*] and this [*they
embrace for the third time*] be the greatest discord
our hearts shall ever know!

Iago   [*aside*] Oh, it's all sweet music now, but I'll
untune your strings, for all my honesty!

Othello   Come, let's go to the castle. News, friends:
the war is over. The Turks are drowned. How are
my old island friends? [*To* **Desdemona**] Darling, you
will be welcomed in Cyprus; I have many good
friends here. Oh my sweet: I chatter on too much,
wallowing in my own contentment. Good Iago, go

Go to the bay and disembark my coffers;
230 Bring thou the Master to the citadel;
He is a good one, and his worthiness
Does challenge much respect. Come, Desdemona,
Once more well met at Cyprus!

[*Exeunt all except* **Iago** *and* **Roderigo**]

Iago   [*to soldiers*] Do thou meet me presently at the
235 harbour. (*To* **Roderigo**) Come hither. If thou be'st
valiant – as, they say, base men being in love have then
a nobility in their natures more than is native to them –
list me. The Lieutenant tonight watches on the court of
guard. First, I must tell thee this: Desdemona is directly
240 in love with him.

Roderigo   With him? Why, 'tis not possible!

Iago   Lay thy finger thus, and let thy soul be instructed.
Mark me with what violence she first loved the Moor,
but for bragging and telling her fantastical lies. And will
245 she love him still for prating? Let not thy discreet heart
think so. Her eye must be fed, and what delight shall
she have to look on the devil? When the blood is made
dull with the act of sport, there should be, again to
inflame it and give satiety a fresh appetite, loveliness in
250 favour, sympathy in years, manners and beauties: all
which the Moor is defective in. Now, for want of these
required conveniences, her delicate tenderness will find
itself abused, begin to heave the gorge, disrelish and
abhor the Moor. Very nature will instruct her to it and
255 compel her to some second choice. Now, sir, this
granted – as it is a most pregnant and unforced
position – who stands so eminently in the degree of this
fortune as Cassio does? – a knave very voluble; no
further conscionable than in putting on the mere form of
260 civil and humane seeming, for the better compassing of

to the bay, will you, and unload my luggage. Bring
the Commander to the castle. He's a good fellow,
and deserves respect. Come, Desdemona. Once
again, it's good to be with you in Cyprus!

[*Everyone leaves except* **Iago** *and* **Roderigo**]

Iago   [*to soldiers, as they march off*] Meet me right
away at the harbour. [*To* **Roderigo**] Come here. If
you have guts – and they say that ordinary men
have more nobility in their natures when they're in
love than they normally do – listen to me. Tonight,
the Lieutenant is on guard duty. First, I have to tell
you this: Desdemona is plainly in love with him.

Roderigo   With him? Why, that's impossible!

Iago   Put your finger here [*he indicates his lips*] and
learn something. Note how passionately she first
loved the Moor, just for bragging and telling her
fantastic lies. Will she continue to love him for his
boasting? Don't you believe it! She's got a visual
appetite. What pleasure can she get from looking at
the devil? When the sex urge cools, to rekindle
desire and give it renewed vigour there should be
attractive appearance, similarity in age, habits and
good looks – all of which the Moor is lacking in.
Now because he does not have these vital qualities,
her sense of delicacy will be affronted. She'll begin
to feel nauseated; detest and loathe the Moor.
Natural instincts will do this to her and compel her
to seek a second choice. Now, sir, grant this – and
it's undeniable – who is more obviously qualified
than Cassio? A smooth talker, who doesn't scruple
to affect civility and politeness in order to

his salt and hidden affections: a subtle slippery knave, a
finder out of occasions; that has an eye can stamp and
counterfeit advantages, though true advantage never
present itself. A devilish knave! Besides, the knave is
265   handsome, young, and hath all those requisites in him
that folly and green minds look after. A pestilent
complete knave; and the woman has found him already.

Roderigo   I cannot believe that in her; she's full of most
blessed condition.

270 **Iago**   Blessed fig's end! The wine she drinks is made of
grapes. If she had been blessed, she would never have
loved the Moor. Blessed pudding! Didst thou not see her
paddle with the palm of his hand? Didst not mark that?

Roderigo   Yes, that I did. But that was but courtesy.

275 **Iago**   Lechery, by this hand! An index and obscure
prologue to the history of lust and foul thoughts. They
met so near with their lips that their breaths embraced
together. Villainous thoughts, Roderigo! When these
mutualities so marshal the way, hard at hand comes the
280   master and main exercise, the incorporate conclusion.
But, sir, be you ruled by me. I have brought you from
Venice. Watch you tonight; for the command, I'll lay't
upon you. Cassio knows you not; I'll not be far from
you. Do you find some occasion to anger Cassio, either
285   by speaking too loud, or tainting his discipline, or from
what other course you please, which the time shall more
favourably minister.

Roderigo   Well.

accomplish his lecherous and secret designs. He's a slippery and subtle wretch; an opportunist, who has an instinct for seeing chances where there really are none. A devilish rogue. Besides, the rogue is handsome, young, with all the qualities sought after by foolish and inexperienced minds. He's an utter and complete rogue, and the woman has picked him out already.

Roderigo   I can't believe she's like that. She's so perfect.

Iago   Perfect, my foot! Her head can be turned like anyone else. If she'd been perfect, she would never have fallen in love with the Moor. Perfect indeed! Didn't you see her fondle the palm of his hand? Didn't you notice that?

Roderigo   Yes, I did, but that was only out of politeness.

Iago   It was lechery, if ever I've seen it. A prologue to a story of lust and obscene thought. Their lips were so close to touching that their breaths embraced. Wicked thoughts, Roderigo! When these familiarities point the way forward, in no time they reach the main purpose of it all: intercourse! Do as I say, sir. I've brought you from Venice. Keep watch tonight: I'll tell you the signal. Cassio doesn't know you. I'll not be far away. Get Cassio angry, by speaking too loud, or sneering at his military skill, or whatever suits you best, according to the circumstances.

Roderigo   Right.

Iago   Sir, he is rash and very sudden in choler, and haply
290   with his truncheon may strike at you; provoke him that
he may, for even out of that will I cause these of Cyprus
to mutiny, whose qualification shall come into no true
taste again, but by the displanting of Cassio. So shall
you have a shorter journey to your desires by the means
295   I shall then have to prefer them, and the impediment
most profitably removed, without which there were no
expectation of our prosperity.

Roderigo   I will do this, if you can bring it to any
opportunity.

300 **Iago**   I warrant thee. Meet me by and by at the citadel. I
must fetch his necessaries ashore. Farewell.

Roderigo   Adieu.

                                                              [*Exit*]

Iago   That Cassio loves her, I do well believe it.
That she loves him, 'tis apt and of great credit.
305   The Moor, howbeit that I endure him not,
Is of a constant, loving, noble nature,
And, I dare think, he'll prove to Desdemona
A most dear husband. Now, I do love her too;
Not out of absolute lust – though peradventure
310   I stand accountant for as great a sin –
But partly led to diet my revenge
For that I do suspect the lustful Moor
Hath leaped into my seat, the thought whereof
Doth, like a poisonous mineral, gnaw my inwards,
315   And nothing can, nor shall, content my soul
Till I am evened with him, wife for wife;
Or failing so, yet that I put the Moor,
At least, into a jealousy so strong
That judgement cannot cure. Which thing to do

Iago   Sir, he's very hasty-tempered and may lash out at you with his baton. Provoke him so that he does. That'll be all I need to get some of the Cyprus garrison to cause a rumpus: the ones who stand no chance of promotion till Cassio goes. That way you'll achieve your objectives all the quicker, because I'll be better able to help you when he's out of the way. We've little chance of success otherwise.

Roderigo   I'll do it if you can fix things up.

Iago   Leave it to me. Meet me soon at the castle. I must fetch his luggage ashore. Farewell.

Roderigo   Adieu!

[*He goes*]

Iago   I really believe Cassio is in love with her. That she loves him is natural and understandable. The Moor – for all that I can't stand him – has a faithful, loving and noble nature, and I dare say he'll prove a good husband to Desdemona. Now, I love her too! Not out of absolute lust – though I'm guilty of something just as sinful – but partly in order to feed my revenge, because I suspect the randy Moor has slept with my wife. The thought of that gripes my innards like a dose of poison! I'll not rest till I get even with him, wife for wife. Failing that, the least I can do is make the Moor insanely jealous. To do

320   If this poor trash of Venice, whom I trash
      For his quick hunting, stand the putting on,
      I'll have our Michael Cassio on the hip,
      Abuse him to the Moor in the rank garb –
      For I fear Cassio with my night-cap too –
325   Make the Moor thank me, love me, and reward me
      For making him egregiously an ass,
      And practising upon his peace and quiet,
      Even to madness. 'Tis here, but yet confused:
      Knavery's plain face is never seen, till used.

                                                    [*Exit*]

Scene 2

Cyprus. A Street. Enter a **Herald,** *with a proclamation.*

Herald   It is Othello's pleasure, our noble and valiant
      General, that upon certain tidings now arrived importing
      the mere perdition of the Turkish fleet, every man put
      himself into triumph: some to dance, some to make
5   bonfires, each man to what sport and revels his mind
      leads him. For, besides these beneficial news, it is the
      celebration of his nuptials. So much was his pleasure
      should be proclaimed. All offices are open, and there is
      full liberty of feasting from this present hour of five till
10   the bell have told eleven. Heaven bless the isle of Cyprus
      and our noble General Othello!

                                                    [*Exit*]

this, if this rubbish-heap from Venice [*he means* **Roderigo**] can be egged on – I usually keep him in check! – I'll have our Michael Cassio just where I want him. I'll tell the Moor he's been having it off – I think Cassio's had my wife, too – and make the Moor thank me, love me and reward me for making him an utter ass, and driving him insane. [*He points to his head*] It's all up here, but not yet sorted out. Villainy's best seen in action.

[*He goes*]

Scene 2

A **Herald** *enters with a proclamation.*

Herald   Othello, our noble and valiant General, calls upon everyone to celebrate the news of the total destruction of the Turkish fleet. Dance; light bonfires; each man to whatever amusement and merrymaking appeals to him, because besides these good tidings, it is also the time to celebrate his marriage. This is his express wish. All taverns and eating-places are open, and everyone is at liberty to feast from now, five o'clock, till the curfew bell at eleven. God bless this land of Cyprus and our noble General Othello!

[*He goes*]

Scene 3

Cyprus. A Hall in the castle. Enter **Othello, Desdemona** *and* **Cassio**.

Othello   Good Michael, look you to the guard tonight.
Let's teach ourselves that honourable stop,
Not to outsport discretion.

Cassio   Iago hath direction what to do;
5   But, notwithstanding, with my personal eye
Will I look to it.

Othello   Iago is most honest.
Michael, good night. Tomorrow with your earliest
Let me have speech with you. (*To* **Desdemona**) Come,
10   my dear love,
The purchase made, the fruits are to ensue:
That profit's yet to come 'twixt me and you.
Good night.

[*Exeunt* **Othello** *and* **Desdemona**]

[*Enter* **Iago**]

Cassio   Welcome, Iago. We must to the watch.

15 **Iago**   Not this hour, Lieutenant; 'tis not yet ten o'clock.
Our General cast us thus early for the love of his
Desdemona; who let us not therefore blame. He hath not
yet made wanton the night with her; and she is sport for
Jove.

20 **Cassio**   She is a most exquisite lady.

Iago   And, I'll warrant her, full of game.

Cassio   Indeed, she is a most fresh and delicate creature.

Scene 3

The guardroom of the castle. Enter **Othello,**
Desdemona, Cassio *and Attendants.*

Othello   Michael, make sure we have guards posted
tonight. We must not let our pleasures weaken
security.

Cassio   Iago knows what to do. Nevertheless, I'll
check things myself.

Othello   Iago is most trustworthy. Michael, good
night. At your earliest convenience tomorrow, I'd
like to talk to you. [*To* **Desdemona**] Come, my dear
love. Our vows are made; we two have to
consummate our love. [*To* **Cassio**] Goodnight.

[**Othello, Desdemona** *and their Attendants leave*]

[**Iago** *enters*]

Cassio   Welcome, Iago. We must visit the guard.

Iago   Not now, Lieutenant. It's not yet ten o'clock. Our
General dismissed us early to be with his
Desdemona, but we mustn't blame him. He hasn't
had his night of fun with her yet. She's a dish for
the gods!

Cassio   She's a lovely lady.

Iago   And full of you-know-what, I'll bet!

Cassio   Yes, she is a very sweet and kindly person.

Iago   What an eye she has! Methinks it sounds a parley to
provocation.

25 **Cassio**   An inviting eye, and yet methinks right modest.

Iago   And when she speaks, is it not an alarm to love?

Cassio   She is indeed perfection.

Iago   Well, happiness to their sheets! Come, Lieutenant, I
have a stoup of wine; and here without are a brace of
30   Cyprus gallants that would fain have a measure to the
health of black Othello.

Cassio   Not tonight, good Iago. I have very poor and
unhappy brains for drinking. I could well wish courtesy
would invent some other custom of entertainment.

35 **Iago**   Oh, they are our friends! But one cup; I'll drink for
you.

Cassio   I have drunk but one cup tonight, and that was
craftily qualified too; and behold what innovation it
makes here. I am unfortunate in the infirmity and dare
40   not task my weakness with any more.

Iago   What, man! 'Tis a night of revels; the gallants desire
it.

Cassio   Where are they?

Iago   Here, at the door; I pray you call them in.

45 **Cassio**   I'll do't, but it dislikes me.

[*Exit*]

Iago   What eyes! She's got a real come-hither look!

Cassio   An open look, but a modest one, I think.

Iago   And when she speaks, hasn't she got a sexy voice?

Cassio   She is indeed perfection.

Iago   Well, all happiness to their bed! Come Lieutenant. I've got a jug of wine. Outside there are a couple of Cypriot lads who'd like to drink the health of black Othello.

Cassio   Not tonight, good Iago. I haven't got a head for drink. I wish there were some other way to celebrate.

Iago   Oh, they're friends of ours! Just one glass. I'll make up for you.

Cassio   I've had one drink tonight, and that was diluted with water too, and see how much the worse I am. I'm unfortunate in having this infirmity, and I daren't risk any more.

Iago   What man! It's a celebration night. The young chaps expect it.

Cassio   Where are they?

Iago   Here, outside. Call them in, do!

Cassio   I will, but reluctantly.

[*He goes*]

Iago If I can fasten but one cup upon him,
With that which he hath drunk tonight already,
He'll be as full of quarrel and offence
As my young mistress' dog. Now my sick fool Roderigo,
50 Whom love hath turned almost the wrong side out,
To Desdemona hath tonight caroused
Potations pottle-deep; and he's to watch.
Three lads of Cyprus, noble swelling spirits –
That hold their honours in a wary distance,
55 The very elements of this warlike isle –
Have I tonight flustered with flowing cups,
And they watch too. Now 'mongst this flock of
        drunkards,
Am I to put our Cassio in some action
60 That may offend the isle. But here they come;
If consequence do but approve my dream,
My boat sails freely both with wind and stream.

[*Enter* **Cassio** *with* **Montano** *and Gentlemen, and a
servant with wine*]

Cassio 'Fore God, they have given me a rouse already.

Montano Good faith, a little one; not past a pint, as I am
65 a soldier.

Iago Some wine ho!
[*sings*]
And let me the canakin clink, clink;
And let me the canakin clink;
70 *A soldier's a man*
Oh, man's life's but a span;
Why, then, let a soldier drink.
Some wine, boys!

Cassio 'Fore God, an excellent song.

Iago   If I can get one drink down him, what with the one he's already drunk tonight, he'll be as quarrelsome and aggressive as a pampered dog. Now my doting fool Roderigo, who's turned almost inside out by love, has drunk to Desdemona about two quarts of ale: and he's on guard-duty! Three other Cypriots, really lively fellows, and quick to take offence – typical of this military island – I've got plastered with plenty of drink, and they are on guard too. I'm going to put our Cassio in amongst this flock of drunkards and involve him in a scene the islanders won't like. Here they come. If my dreams come true, my ship's about to come home!

[**Cassio** *enters, the worse for drink, accompanied by* **Montano**, *several* **Gentlemen** *and Servants carrying wine*]

Cassio   By God, they've given me a large glass already!

Montano   'Strewth, only a little one. Not more than a pint, as I'm a soldier!

Iago   Some wine, there!
[*He sings*] *And let me the drinking-cup clink, clink;*
And let me the drinking-cup clink.
   A soldier's a sport
   And life's very short
Why, then, let a soldier drink!
Some wine, boys!

Cassio   By God, that's an excellent song!

75 **Iago** I learned it in England, where indeed they are most
potent in potting. Your Dane, your German, and your
swag-bellied Hollander – drink, ho! – are nothing to
your English.

Cassio Is your Englishman so expert in his drinking?

80 **Iago** Why, he drinks you with facility your Dane dead
drunk; he sweats not to overthrow your Almain; he gives
your Hollander a vomit ere the next pottle can be filled.

Cassio To the health of our General!

Montano I am for it, Lieutenant; and I will do you
85 justice.

Iago Oh, sweet England!
[*sings*]
King Stephen was a worthy peer,
His breeches cost him but a crown;
He held them sixpence all too dear;
90 *With that he called the tailor lown.*
He was a wight of high renown,
And thou art but of low degree;
'Tis pride that pulls the country down;
Then take thine auld cloak about thee.
95 Some wine, ho!

Cassio 'Fore God, this is a more exquisite song than the
other.

Iago Will you hear't again?

Cassio No, for I held him to be unworthy of his place
100 that does those things. Well, God's above all; and there
be souls must be saved, and there be souls must not be
saved.

Iago It is true, good Lieutenant.

Iago   I learned it in England, where they're formidable drinkers. Your Danes, your Germans, and your pot-bellied Dutch – drink up! – are not in the same class as your English.

Cassio   Is your Englishman such an expert drinker?

Iago   Why, he can easily drink your Dane under the table. It's no sweat for him to beat your Kraut. He pauses to let your Dutchman vomit, so there's enough room for his next couple of pints.

Cassio   To the health of our General!

Montano   I'll drink to that, Lieutenant! I'll sink one with you!

Iago   Oh, dear old England!
[*He sings*] *King Stephen was a noble peer;*
He bought his trousers for a song;
He thought the price was much too dear,
And cursed his tailor loud and long.
He was a man of high renown,
And you are of the lowest rank;
'Tis pride that pulls the country down:
Wear your old clothes and do not swank!
Some wine there!

Cassio   [*very drunk now*] By God, this is an even more exquisite song than the other!

Iago   Would you like to hear it again?

Cassio   No; I deplore people who do things like that. Well, God is supreme. Some souls must be saved, and other souls must not be saved . . .

Iago   That's true, good Lieutenant.

Cassio   For mine own part – no offence to the General,
105   nor any man of quality – I hope to be saved.

Iago   And so do I too, Lieutenant.

Cassio   Ay, but by your leave, not before me. The
Lieutenant is to be saved before the Ancient. Let's have
no more of this; let's to our affairs. God forgive us our
110   sins! Gentlemen, let's look to our business. Do not think,
gentlemen, I am drunk; this is my Ancient, this is my
right hand, and this is my left hand. I am not drunk
now; I can stand well enough and I speak well enough.

Gentlemen   Excellent well.

115 **Cassio**   Very well then. You must not think that I am
drunk.

Montano   To the platform, master. Come, let's set the
watch.

[*Exit*]

Iago   You see this fellow that is gone before:
120   He is a soldier fit to stand by Caesar
And give direction; and do but see his vice:
'Tis to his virtue a just equinox,
The one as long as the other. 'Tis pity of him.
I fear the trust Othello puts in him,
125   On some odd time of his infirmity,
Will shake this island.

Montano   But is he often thus?

Iago   'Tis evermore the prologue to his sleep:
He'll watch the horologe a double set,
130   If drink rock not his cradle.

Casio   As for me – no offence to the General, or any gentleman of quality – I hope to be saved.

Iago   And so do I, too, Lieutenant.

Cassio   Yes, but begging your pardon, not before me. A Lieutenant must be saved before a Sergeant. Let's not talk about this any more, let's get down to business. Do not think, gentlemen, that I am drunk. This is my Staff-Sergeant; this is my right hand; and this is my left. I'm not drunk. I can stand all right, and I can speak all right!

Gentlemen   Very well!

Cassio   Yes, very well. You mustn't think I'm drunk, then.

[*He goes*]

Montano   To the battlements, gentlemen. We must go on duty.

Iago   You see that man who's just left? He's a soldier, fit to stand next to Caesar and give orders. Just observe his vice. It balances out his virtue exactly: the one is as great as the other. It's a great pity. I fear that the trust Othello places in him will be the undoing of this island if he happens to be in one of his drunken moods.

Montano   Is he often like this?

Iago   He's the same every night before he goes to bed. He's awake all night if he doesn't have his drink to put him to sleep.

Montano   It were well
The General were put in mind of it:
Perhaps he sees it not, or his good nature
Prizes the virtue that appears in Cassio
135   And looks not on his evils. Is not this true?

[*Enter* **Roderigo**]

Iago   (*aside*) How now, Roderigo?
I pray you after the Lieutenant, go!

[*Exit* **Roderigo**]

Montano   And 'tis great pity that the noble Moor
Should hazard such a place as his own second
140   With one of an ingraft infirmity.
It were an honest action to say
So to the Moor.

Iago   Not I, for this fair island!
I do love Cassio well and would do much
145   To cure him of the evil.

[*Cry within: 'Help! Help!'*]

                                     But hark, what noise?

[*Enter* **Cassio,** *pursuing* **Roderigo**]

Cassio   Zounds, you rogue, you rascal!

Montano   What's the matter, Lieutenant?

Cassio   A knave teach me my duty! I'll beat the knave
150   into a wicker bottle.

Roderigo   Beat me?

Cassio   Dost thou prate, rogue?

[*striking* **Roderigo**]

Montano It would be wise to inform the General.
Perhaps he's never seen it, or his good nature
overlooks Cassio's faults because of his virtues. Isn't
this the case?

[**Roderigo** *enters*]

Iago [*aside*] Right, Roderigo! Follow the Lieutenant –

[**Roderigo** *goes*]

Montano And it's a great pity that the noble Moor
should risk appointing as his second-in-command a
man with a chronic problem. It's only right to say so
to the Moor.

Iago Not me, for all of Cyprus! I like Cassio a lot and
would do anything to cure him of this evil.

[*A cry is heard: 'Help, help!'*]

Listen: what's that?

[**Cassio** *enters, chasing* **Roderigo**]

Cassio God, you rogue! You rascal!

Montano What's the matter, Lieutenant?

Cassio A rogue like him teach me my duty? I'll beat
the rogue into little shreds!

Roderigo Beat me!

Cassio Are you answering me back, you rogue?

[*He strikes* **Roderigo**]

Montano   Good Lieutenant; pray sir, hold your hand.

Cassio   Let me go, sir, or I'll knock you o'er the mazzard.

155 **Montano**   Come, come, you're drunk.

Cassio   Drunk!

[*They fight*]

Iago   (*to* **Roderigo**) Away, I say! Go out and cry a mutiny.

[*Exit* **Roderigo**]

Nay, good Lieutenant. God's will, gentleman!
Help, ho! Lieutenant! Sir! Montano! Sir!
160   Help, masters. Here's a goodly watch indeed.

[*A bell rings*]

Who's that which rings the bell? Diablo, ho!
The town will rise. God's will, Lieutenant, hold!
You will be shamed for ever!

[*Enter* **Othello** *and Attendants*]

Othello   What is the matter here?

165 **Montano**   Zounds, I bleed still.
I am hurt to the death.

Othello   Hold for your lives!

Iago   Hold, hold, Lieutenant, sir, Montano, gentlemen!
Have you forgot all sense of place and duty?
170   Hold! The General speaks to you: hold, hold, for shame!

Othello   Why, how now, ho! From whence ariseth this?
Are we turned Turks and to ourselves do that
Which heaven hath forbid the Ottomites?
For Christian shame, put by this barbarous brawl.

Montano Now good Lieutenant! Do restrain yourself!

[*He takes* **Cassio** *by the arm*]

Cassio Let me go, sir, or I'll bash you over the head.

Montano Come, come. You're drunk.

Cassio Drunk! [*He scuffles with* **Montano**. *They both draw their swords*]

Iago [*To* **Roderigo**] Go, I tell you, Raise all hell.

[**Roderigo** *leaves*]

Now, good Lieutenant! For heaven's sake, sir! Help!
Lieutenant! Sir! Montano! Sir! Help, gentlemen!
This is a fine sort of guard-duty!

[*An alarm bell rings, adding to the panic and confusion*]

Who's ringing that bell? The devil! The town will be
in an uproar.
For God's sake, Lieutenant, stop! You'll be
disgraced forever!

[**Othello** *enters with attendants*]

Othello What's going on here?

Montano God, I'm still bleeding! I'm done for!

Othello Stop, on pain of death!

Iago Stop, Lieutenant, sir! Montano! Gentlemen!
Have you forgotten all sense of your rank and duty?
Stop! The General is speaking to you! Stop, for
shame!

Othello Now then, now then! What started this? Have
we all turned Turks, doing to ourselves what God
has denied to them? For Christian shame, stop this

175　He that stirs next to carve for his own rage
　　　Holds his soul light: he dies upon his motion.
　　　Silence that dreadful bell; it frights the isle
　　　From her propriety. What is the matter, masters?
　　　Honest Iago, that looks dead with grieving,
180　Speak, who began this? On thy love I charge thee.

Iago   I do not know. Friends all but now, even now;
　　　In quarter and in terms like bride and groom
　　　Devesting them for bed: and then but now,
　　　As if some planet had unwitted men,
185　Swords out, and tilting one at others' breasts
　　　In opposition bloody. I cannot speak
　　　Any beginning to this peevish odds;
　　　And would in action glorious I had lost
　　　These legs that brought me to a part of it.

190 **Othello**   How came it, Michael, you were thus forgot?

Cassio   I pray you pardon me: I cannot speak.

Othello   Worthy Montano, you were wont to be civil:
　　　The gravity and stillness of your youth
　　　The world hath noted; and your name is great
195　In mouths of wisest censure. What's the matter
　　　That you unlace your reputation thus
　　　And spend your rich opinion for the name
　　　Of a night-brawler? Give me answer to it.

Montano   Worthy Othello, I am hurt to danger.
200　Your officer, Iago, can inform you,
　　　While I spare speech, which something now offends me,
　　　Of all that I do know; nor know I aught
　　　By me that's said or done amiss this night,
　　　Unless self-charity be sometimes a vice,
205　And to defend ourselves it be a sin
　　　When violence assails us.

barbarous brawling. The next to strike a blow holds his life cheap: one move and he's dead. Silence that mournful bell: it's upsetting the whole island. What is the matter, gentlemen? Honest Iago, who looks dead with grief, speak! Who began this? Answer, if you love me!

Iago   I do not know. Until just now – a moment ago – friends on duty, their relationship like that of a bride and groom undressing for bed. Then all of a sudden – as if driven mad by a malign star – their swords were out and they were duelling in deadly earnest. I can't say how this senseless quarrel started. Would these legs that took me to it had been lost in glorious battle!

Othello   Michael, how did you come to forget yourself like this?

Cassio   Forgive me. I can't speak.

Othello   Worthy Montano: you are usually well-behaved. The serious and sober nature of your youth has been widely noted. You are well regarded amongst the shrewd. What has happened that you should ruin your reputation like this and exchange your good name for that of a hooligan? Your answer?

Montano   Worthy Othello, I am seriously wounded. Your officer, Iago, can tell you everything I know to save me talking, which hurts. I know of nothing that I have said or done amiss tonight, unless looking after oneself can be called a vice, and it is a sin to defend oneself when attacked.

Othello   Now, by heaven,
My blood begins my safer guides to rule,
And passion, having my best judgement collied
210 Assays to lead the way. Zounds, if I stir,
Or do but lift this arm, the best of you
Shall sink in my rebuke. Give me to know
How this foul rout began, who set it on;
And he that is approved in this offence,
215 Though he had twinned with me, both at a birth,
Shall lose me. What! In a town of war
Yet wild, the people's hearts brimful of fear,
To manage private and domestic quarrels
In night, and on the court and guard of safety?
220 'Tis monstrous. Iago, who began it?

Montano   If partially affined or leagued in office,
Thou dost deliver more or less than truth,
Thou art no soldier.

Iago   Touch me not so near.
225 I had rather have this tongue cut from my mouth
Than it should do offence to Michael Cassio.
Yet, I persuade myself, to speak the truth
Shall nothing wrong him. This it is, General.
Montano and myself being in speech,
230 There comes a fellow, crying out for help,
And Cassio following with determined sword
To execute upon him. Sir, this gentleman
Steps in to Cassio and entreats his pause:
Myself the crying fellow did pursue
235 Lest by his clamour – as it so fell out –
The town might fall in fright. He, swift of foot,
Outran my purpose; and I returned the rather
For that I heard the clink and fall of swords
And Cassio high in oaths, which till tonight
240 I ne'er might say before. When I came back –

Othello   Now, by heaven, I'm beginning to lose my
temper, and anger is obscuring my better
judgement. God, if I so much as move or lift my
sword, the best of you will die! Tell me how this
disgraceful brawl began. Who started it? The guilty
one, even if he's my twin brother – I'll have done
with him! What? In a garrison town, still under
threat – the people jittery – to instigate a private and
personal quarrel at night in the guardroom when on
watch? It's monstrous! Iago, who began it?

Montano   If you do not tell the whole truth – because
you are biased, or afraid to testify against a superior
officer – you are no soldier!

Iago   I'm well aware of that. I'd rather have my
tongue cut out than use it to accuse Michael Cassio.
On the other hand, I tell myself, it can do him no
harm to tell the truth. This is it, General. Montano
and I were talking. A fellow arrives, crying out for
help, with Cassio chasing him with drawn sword,
intent on using it. Sir, this gentleman [**Iago** *indicates*
Montano] intercedes with Cassio, and begs him to
stop. I pursued the fellow who was making the fuss
in case – as actually happened – the town took
fright. Being nimble-footed he outran me, and I
returned, because I heard the clash of swords and
Cassio cursing loudly: something I could never say
about him till tonight. When I came back – it didn't

113

For this was brief – I found them close together
At blow and thrust, even as again they were
When you yourself did part them.
More of this matter can I not report:
245 But men are men; the best sometimes forget.
Though Cassio did some little wrong to him,
As men in rage strike those that wish them best,
Yet surely Cassio, I believe, received
From him that fled some strange indignity
250 Which patience could not pass.

Othello   I know, Iago,
Thy honesty and love doth mince this matter,
Making it light to Cassio. Cassio, I love thee,
But nevermore be officer of mine.

[*Enter* **Desdemona**, *attended*]

255 Look, if my gentle love be not raised up!
I'll make thee an example.

Desdemona   What is the matter, dear?

Othello   All's well now, sweeting: come away to bed.
Sir, for your hurts myself will be your surgeon.

[**Montano** *is led off*]

260 Iago, look with care about the town
And silence those whom this vile brawl distracted.
Come, Desdemona, 'tis the solders' life
To have their balmy slumbers waked with strife.

[*Exeunt all but* **Iago** *and* **Cassio**]

Iago   What, are you hurt, Lieutenant?

265 **Cassio**   Ay, past all surgery.

Iago   Marry, God forbid!

take long – I found them hard at it, cutting and thrusting, just as they were when you parted them yourself. I can tell you no more. Men are men. The best sometimes forget themselves. Though Cassio wronged him a little – angry men often strike those who are on their side – yet I believe Cassio must have received an insufferable insult from the man who fled.

Othello   I know, Iago, that your honesty and your love make you play this matter down, to let Cassio off lightly. Cassio, I love you: but you shall never be an officer of mine again.

[**Desdemona** *enters with her Attendants*]

Look; my gentle love has been disturbed. [*To* **Cassio**] I'll make an example of you.

Desdemona   What's the matter, dear?

Othello   All's well now, my sweet. Come to bed. [*To* **Montano**] Sir, I'll tend your wounds myself.

[**Montano** *is led off*]

Iago, check the town carefully. Silence those who've been excited by this disgraceful brawl. Come, Desdemona; it's a soldier's life, having sweet sleep broken by brawls.

[*Everyone leaves except* **Iago** *and* **Cassio**]

Iago   Are you hurt, Lieutenant?

Cassio   Yes, past all surgery.

Iago   Oh, God forbid!

Cassio   Reputation, reputation! Oh, I have lost my
reputation! I have lost the immortal part, sir, of myself,
and what remains is bestial. My reputation, Iago, my
270   reputation!

Iago   As I am an honest man I thought you had received
some bodily wound: there is more of sense in that than
in reputation. Reputation is an idle and most false
imposition; oft got without merit and lost without
275   deserving. You have lost no reputation at all, unless you
repute yourself such a loser. What, man! There are ways
to recover the General again. You are but now cast in
his mood – a punishment more in policy than in malice –
even so as one would beat his offenceless dog to affright
280   an imperious lion. Sue to him again, and he's yours.

Cassio   I will rather sue to be despised than to deceive so
good a commander with so slight, so drunken, and so
indiscreet an officer. Drunk! And speak parrot! And
squabble! Swagger! Swear! And discourse fustian with
285   one's own shadow! Oh, thou invisible spirit of wine, if
thou hast no name to be known by, let us call thee devil!

Iago   What was he that you followed with your sword?
What had he done to you?

Cassio   I know not.

290 **Iago**   Is't possible?

Cassio   I remember a mass of things, but nothing
distinctly: a quarrel, but nothing wherefore. Oh God,
that men should put an enemy in their mouths to steal
away their brains! That we should with joy, pleasure,
295   revel and applause transform ourselves into beasts!

Cassio   Reputation, reputation! Oh, I've lost my reputation! I've lost my very soul, sir, and what remains is bestial. My reputation, Iago, my reputation!

Iago   I honestly thought you'd received some physical hurt. That would make more sense than worrying about reputation. Reputation is a useless and misleading burden: often got without merit and lost undeservedly. You've lost no reputation at all, unless it's to yourself. What, man? There are ways of getting back in favour again with the General. You're just a victim of his mood. It's a punishment of principle rather than of malice: the kind that clobbers the innocent to frighten the would-be criminal. Plead with him again, and he'll forgive you.

Cassio   I'd rather plead to be despised than betray so fine a commander with so worthless, so drunken, so indiscreet an officer! Drunk! Talking rubbish! Brawling! Throwing my weight around! Swearing! And talking big to my own shadow! Oh, the invisible spirit that lurks in wine: it's devilish!

Iago   Who were you chasing with your sword? What had he done to you?

Cassio   I don't know.

Iago   How can that be?

Cassio   I remember things in general but nothing distinctly. A quarrel, but not the reason for it. Oh God, that men should let their tongues be their enemy, to run off with their brains! That we should transform ourselves into beasts through joy, delight, revelry and the pursuit of popularity!

Iago   Why, but you are now well enough! How came you thus recovered?

Cassio   It hath pleased the devil drunkenness to give place to the devil wrath: one unperfectness shows me another, 300 to make me frankly despise myself.

Iago   Come, you are too severe a moraler. As the time, the place and the condition of this country stands, I could heartily wish this had not so befallen; but since it is as it is, mend it, for your own good.

305 **Cassio**   I will ask him for my place again; he shall tell me I am a drunkard. Had I as many mouths as Hydra, such an answer would stop them all. To be now a sensible man, by and by a fool, and presently a beast! Oh, strange! Every inordinate cup is unblessed and the 310 ingredience is a devil.

Iago   Come, come; good wine is a good familiar creature if it be well used; exclaim no more against it. And, good Lieutenant, I think you think I love you.

Cassio   I have well approved it, sir. I drunk!

315 **Iago**   You or any man living may be drunk at some time, man. I'll tell you what you shall do. Our General's wife is now the General. I may say so in this respect, for that he hath devoted and given up himself to the contemplation, mark, and devotement of her parts and 320 graces. Confess yourself freely to her; importune her help to put you in your place again. She is of so free, so kind, so apt, so blessed a disposition, that she holds it a vice in her goodness not to do more than she is requested. This broken joint between you and her husband, entreat 325 her to splinter; and my fortunes against any lay worth naming, this crack of your love shall grow stronger than it was before.

Iago   But you are all right now. How did you recover so quickly?

Cassio   The devil of drunkenness has yielded place to the devil of anger. One imperfection leads to another to make me utterly despise myself.

Iago   Come on, you are too hard on yourself! As this country stands at present, I wish most heartily this hadn't happened. But since it has, get over it for your own good.

Cassio   I'll ask to be reinstated; he'll tell me I'm a drunkard. If I had as many mouths as Hydra had heads, an answer like that would shut them all. To be first a sensible man, next a fool, and finally a beast! Oh, how weird! Every excessive tankard is cursed and the contents devilish.

Iago   Oh, come. Good wine is a friendly spirit if it's properly used. Don't say another word against it. And, good Lieutenant, I think you know I'm a good friend of yours.

Cassio   I've good reason to think so. Me, drunk!

Iago   You or any living man could be drunk at some time, man! I'll tell you what to do. Our General's wife wears the trousers. I say this because he has devoted and dedicated himself to contemplating, noting and worshipping her personal qualities and charms. Open your heart to her. Beg her help in getting yourself reinstated. She's so open, so kind, so willing, so sweet, that she feels guilty if she isn't doing more than is expected of her. This fracture between you and her husband: ask her to mend it. I'll bet all I've got against any odds that this breach in your love will make it stronger than it was before.

Cassio   You advise me well.

Iago   I protest in the sincerity of love and honest kindness.

330 **Cassio**   I think it freely, and betimes in the morning I will
    beseech the virtuous Desdemona to undertake for me. I
    am desperate of my fortunes if they check me here.

Iago   You are in the right. Good night, Lieutenant, I must
    to the watch.

335 **Cassio**   Good night, honest Iago.

                                                        [*Exit*]

Iago   And what's he then that says I play the villain,
        When this advice is free I give, and honest,
        Probal to thinking, and indeed the course
        To win the Moor again? For 'tis most easy
340   The inclining Desdemona to subdue
        In any honest suit. She's framed as fruitful
        As the free elements; and then for her
        To win the Moor, were't to renounce his baptism,
        All seals and symbols of redeemed sin,
345   His soul is so enfettered to her love,
        That she may make, unmake, do what she list,
        Even as her appetite shall play the god
        With his weak function. How am I then a villain
        To counsel Cassio to this parallel course
350   Directly to his good? Divinity of hell!
        When devils will their blackest sins put on,
        They do suggest at first with heavenly shows
        As I do now. For while this honest fool
        Plies Desdemona to repair his fortunes
355   And she for him pleads strongly to the Moor,
        I'll pour this pestilence into his ear:

Cassio   That's good advice.

Iago   It's offered in all the sincerity of love and honest kindness.

Cassio   I'm sure it is. Early tomorrow morning I'll beg the virtuous Desdemona to take my case up. I'm ruined if I'm sacked now.

Iago   Too true. Goodnight, Lieutenant. I must go on duty.

Cassio   Goodnight, honest Iago.

[*He goes*]

Iago   Who says I'm playing the villain, when I give free advice that is honest, perfectly reasonable, and indeed the way to win the Moor's respect again? It's very easy to persuade the sympathetic Desdemona to support a good cause. She's all generosity. She could win over the Moor: he's so shackled by his love for her she can make him do, or not do, whatever she wishes, even to renouncing his faith and hopes of salvation, so much does his infatuation for her dominate his reason. How can I be a villain, then, to advise Cassio to do what suits us both when it is directly to his advantage? The theology of Hell! When devils are at their most sinful work, like me they first present themselves as angels. When this honest fool appeals to Desdemona to repair his fortunes, and she strongly pleads on his behalf to the Moor, I'll pour this

That she repeals him for her body's lust,
And by how much she strives to do him good,
She shall undo her credit with the Moor.
360   So will I turn her virtue into pitch,
And out of her own goodness make the net
That shall enmesh them all.

[*Enter* **Roderigo**]

How now, Roderigo?

Roderigo   I do follow here in the chase, not like a hound
365   that hunts, but one that fills up the cry. My money is
almost spent; I have been tonight exceedingly well
cudgelled; and I think the issue will be, I shall have so
much experience for my pains; and so, with no money at
all, and a little more wit, return again to Venice.

370   **Iago**   How poor are they that have not patience!
What wound did ever heal but by degrees?
Thou know'st we work by wit, and not by witchcraft,
And wit depends on dilatory time.
Does't not go well? Cassio hath beaten thee,
375   And thou by that small hurt hath cashiered Cassio.
Though other things grow fair against the sun,
Yet fruits that blossom first will first be ripe.
Content thyself awhile. By the mass, 'tis morning;
Pleasure and action make the hours seem short.
380   Retire thee; go where thou art billeted.
Away, I say, thou shalt know more hereafter:
Nay, get thee gone.

[*Exit* **Roderigo**]

Two things are to be done.
My wife must move for Cassio to her mistress:
I'll set her on.

poison into his ear: that she wants him restored to satisfy her lust. By the extent to which she strives to do him good, she'll correspondingly discredit herself with the Moor. That way I'll convert her virtue into vice, and out of her own goodness make the net that will enmesh them all.

[**Roderigo** *enters*]

Well, Roderigo?

Roderigo   I'm in this hunt not as the front runner, but as a mere member of the pack. I'm almost bankrupt; I've been thoroughly beaten up tonight; and I think the outcome will be that I'll have nothing for my pains but experience. So, broke but wiser, I'll return to Venice.

Iago   How poor are those who lack patience! What wound ever healed otherwise than slowly? You know we work with our wits, not by witchcraft, and brainwork needs plenty of time. Aren't things going well? Cassio has thrashed you; and as a result of that small hurt, Cassio has been cashiered. And though everything seems sunny with Desdemona and Othello, what blossoms first also ripens first: just bide your time. By heavens, it's morning! Time flies when you are enjoying yourself and doing things. Off to bed with you; go to your lodgings. Away, I tell you: you'll learn more later. No: off you go!

[**Roderigo** *goes*]

Two things are to be done. My wife must plead with Desdemona on behalf of Cassio. I'll get her to do

385   Myself the while to draw the Moor apart,
And bring him jump when he may Cassio fi) d
Soliciting his wife. Ay, that's the way.
Dull not device by coldness and delay

[Exit]

this. Meanwhile, I myself will draw the Moor to one
side, and take him to the spot where he'll see
Cassio pleading with his wife. Yes, that's the way.
One shouldn't spoil plans by letting them go cold.

[*He goes*]

Act three

Scene 1

Cyprus: before the Castle. Enter **Cassio** *and Musicians.*

Cassio   Masters, play here – I will content your pains –
Something that's brief; and bid 'Good morrow, General'.

[*Music*]

[*Enter* **Clown**]

Clown   Why, masters, have your instruments been in
Naples, that they speak i'the nose thus?

5 **1st Musician**   How, sir, how?

Clown   Are these, I pray you, wind instruments?

1st Musician   Ay, marry are they, sir.

Clown   Oh, thereby hangs a tail.

1st Musician   Whereby hangs a tale, sir?

10 **Clown**   Marry, sir, by many a wind instrument, that I
know. But, masters, here's money for you; and the
General so likes your music that he desires you, for love's
sake, to make no more noise with it.

1st Musician   Well, sir, we will not.

15 **Clown**   If you have any music that may not be heard, to it
again. But, as they say, to hear music the General does
not greatly care.

Act three

Scene 1

Daybreak. **Cassio** *enters with Musicians; it was the custom to serenade newlyweds at dawn.*

Cassio Gentlemen, play here. I'll settle the bill. Something short. Say 'Good morning, General'.

[*The Musicians play. A* **Clown** *enters*]

Clown Gentlemen, have your instruments been to Naples? [*Naples was infamous for venereal disease*] They sound as though they've caught a dose.

1st Musician In what way, sir?

Clown Are these, begging your pardon, wind instruments?

1st Musician Yes, indeed they are, sir.

Clown Ah. Thereby hangs a tail!

1st Musician What tale hangs where, sir?

Clown Close to many a wind instrument, I know that. Gentlemen, here's some money for you. The General likes your music so much that he requests you, for love's sake, to make no more noise.

1st Musician Well sir, we won't.

Clown If you've any music that's silent, continue. But, as they say, (*he affects a posh voice*] to hear music . . . the General . . . does not . . . greatly . . . care.

1st Musician We have none such, sir.

Clown Then put your pipes in your bag, for I'll away.
20   Go, vanish into air! Away!

[*Exeunt* **Musicians**]

Cassio Dost thou hear, my honest friend?

Clown No, I hear not your honest friend: I hear you.

Cassio Prithee keep up thy quillets. There's a poor piece
of gold for thee. If the gentlewoman that attends the
25   General's wife be stirring, tell her there's one Cassio
entreats her a little favour of speech. Wilt thou do this?

Clown She is stirring, sir. If she will stir hither, I shall
seem to notify unto her.

Cassio Do, good my friend.

[*Exit* **Clown**]

[*Enter* **Iago**]

30   In happy time, Iago.

Iago   You have not been abed then?

Cassio Why, no, the day had broke before we parted.
I have made bold, Iago,
To send in to your wife. My suit to her
35   Is that she will to virtuous Desdemona
Procure me some access.

Iago   I'll send her to you presently;
And I'll devise a mean to draw the Moor
Out of the way, that your converse and business
40   May be more free.

Cassio   I humbly thank you for it.

[*Exit* **Iago**]

1st Musician   We haven't got any silent music, sir.

Clown   Then stick your pipes in your bag. [*He sings a line from a popular song*] 'For I'll away'. Go. Vanish into air. Away!

[*The* **Musicians** *go*]

Cassio   Do you hear, my honest friend?

Clown   I can't hear your honest friend. I can hear you.

Cassio   Keep up the wisecracks. There's a small tip for you. If the gentlewoman who waits on the General's wife is up and around, tell her there's someone called Cassio who'd like a quick word with her. Will you do this?

Clown   She is up and around, sir. If she'll 'up and around' here, (*posh voice again*] I shall tell her.

Cassio   Do, my good friend.

[*The* **Clown** *goes*]

[**Iago** *enters*]

Well met.

Iago   You haven't been to bed, then?

Cassio   Why no. Dawn had broken before we parted. I've taken the liberty, Iago, to send a message in to your wife. I'm going to ask her to use her influence to get me an audience with Desdemona.

Iago   I'll send her to you immediately. And I'll think of something to get the Moor out of the way so you can talk and discuss business more freely.

Cassio   I'm very grateful.

[**Iago** *goes*]

I never knew a Florentine more kind and honest.

[*Enter* **Emilia**]

Emilia   Good morrow, good Lieutenant; I am sorry
For your displeasure: but all will sure be well.
45   The General and his wife are talking of it,
And she speaks for you stoutly. The Moor replies
That he you hurt is of great fame in Cyprus,
And great affinity; and that in wholesome wisdom
He might not but refuse you; but he protests he loves you
50   And needs no other suitor but his likings
To take the safest occasion by the front
To bring you in again.

Cassio   Yet I beseech you,
If you think fit, or that it may be done,
55   Give me advantage of some brief discourse
With Desdemona alone.

Emilia   Pray you, come in:
I will bestow you where you shall have time
To speak your bosom freely.

60   **Cassio**   I am much bound to you

[*Exeunt*]

I never knew a Florentine more kind and honest.

[**Emilia** *enters*]

Emilia   Good morning, good Lieutenant. I'm sorry to hear of your trouble, but all will come right in the end. The General and his wife are discussing it, and she's speaking up for you stoutly. The Moor replies that the man you hurt is very well known in Cyprus, and very well connected, and that politically speaking he has no alternative but to refuse you. But he insists that he's very fond of you and needs no other advocate but his own liking of you to take the first safe occasion to re-appoint you.

Cassio   Nevertheless I would ask you, if you think it's all right and can be arranged, to let me have a brief word with Desdemona, alone.

Emilia   Please come in. I'll find somewhere where you can talk freely.

Cassio   I'm much obliged to you.

[*They go in*]

Scene 2

Cyprus. The Castle. Enter **Othello, Iago** *and Gentlemen.*

Othello   These letters give, Iago, to the pilot,
And by him do my duties to the senate.
That done, I will be walking on the works;
Repair there to me.

5 **Iago**   Well, my good lord, I'll do't.

Othello   This fortification, gentlemen, shall we see it?

Gentlemen   We wait upon your lordship.

[Exeunt]

Scene 3

Cyprus. The garden of the Castle. Enter **Desdemona, Cassio** *and* **Emilia.**

Desdemona   Be thou assured, good Cassio, I will do
All my abilities in thy behalf.

Emilia   Good madam, do. I warrant it grieves my husband
As if the case were his.

5 **Desdemona**   Oh, that's an honest fellow! Do not doubt, Cassio,
But I will have my lord and you again
As friendly as you were.

Scene 2

Othello *has been writing despatches home. He enters with* **Iago** *and a Gentleman.*

Othello   Iago, give these letters to the ship's pilot. Ask him to convey my respects to the Senate. That done, I'll be touring the defences. Meet me there.

Iago   Certainly my good lord. I'll do that.

[*He goes*]

Othello   The defences, gentlemen. Shall we inspect them?

Gentlemen   At your lordship's pleasure . . .

[*They go*]

Scene 3

Desdemona's *private suite.* **Desdemona, Cassio** *and* **Emilia** *are in conference.*

Desdemona   Be assured, good Cassio, I'll do all I can on your behalf.

Emilia   Good madam, do. I know it grieves my husband as if the trouble were his own.

Desdemona   Oh he's an honest fellow! Do not doubt, Cassio, that I'll have my lord and you good friends again.

Cassio   Bounteous madam,
      Whatever shall become of Michael Cassio,
10   He's never anything but your true servant.

Desdemona   I know it. I thank you. You do love my lord;
      You have known him long, and be you well assured
      He shall in strangeness stand no farther off
      Than in a politic distance.

15 **Cassio**   Ay, but, lady,
      That policy may either last so long,
      Or feed upon such nice and waterish diet,
      Or breed itself so out of circumstance,
      That, I being absent and my place supplied,
20   My General will forget my love and service.

Desdemona   Do not doubt that. Before Emilia here,
      I give thee warrant of thy place. Assure thee,
      If I do vow a friendship, I'll perform it
      To the last article. My lord shall never rest.
25   I'll watch him tame, and talk him out of patience;
      His bed shall seem a school, his board a shrift;
      I'll intermingle everything he does
      With Cassio's suit. Therefore be merry, Cassio,
      For thy solicitor shall rather die
30   Than give thy cause away.

      [*Enter* **Othello** *and* **Iago**]

Emilia   Madam, here comes my lord.

Cassio   Madam, I'll take my leave.

Desdemona   Why, stay and hear me speak.

Cassio   Madam, not now; I am very ill at ease,
35   Unfit for mine own purpose.

Desdemona   Well, do your discretion.

                                    [*Exit* **Cassio**]

Cassio   Most generous madam: whatever may happen to Michael Cassio, he will always be your faithful servant.

Desdemona   I know that. I thank you. You love my lord. You have known him a long time. You can be sure that he'll be estranged no longer than is good policy.

Cassio   Yes, but lady: that 'policy' may either go on so long, or weaken so much, or become so inappropriate that – in my absence and with my post occupied – my General will forget my love and service.

Desdemona   Don't worry about that. Emilia is my witness that I guarantee your post. Be assured that if I commit myself in friendship, I'll do things thoroughly. My lord won't rest. I'll keep him awake; talk him out of patience; his bed will seem like a school; his table a confessional; I'll bring Cassio's case into everything he does. So cheer up, Cassio! Your advocate would rather die than abandon your cause.

[**Othello** *and* **Iago** *enter*]

Emilia   Madam, here comes my lord.

Cassio   Madam, I'll go now.

Desdemona   Why? Stay and hear me speak.

Cassio   Madam, not now. I am very embarrassed; not at my best.

Desdemona   Well, as you think right.

[**Cassio** *leaves*]

Iago   Ha! I like not that.

Othello   What dost thou say?

Iago   Nothing, my lord; or if – I know not what.

40 **Othello**   Was not that Cassio parted from my wife?

Iago   Cassio, my lord? No, sure, I cannot think it
      That he would sneak away so guilty-like,
      Seeing you coming.

Othello   I do believe 'twas he.

45 **Desdemona**   How now, my lord?
      I have been talking with a suitor here,
      A man that languishes in your displeasure.

Othello   Who is't you mean?

Desdemona   Why, your Lieutenant, Cassio. Good my
50   lord,
      If I have any grace or power to move you,
      His present reconciliation take.
      For if he be not one that truly loves you,
      That errs in ignorance, and not in cunning,
55   I have no judgement in an honest face.
      I prithee call him back.

Othello   Went he hence now?

Desdemona   Yes, faith; so humbled
      That he hath left part of his grief with me
60   To suffer with him. Good love, call him back.

Othello   Not now, sweet Desdemona. Some other time.

Desdemona   But shall't be shortly?

Othello   The sooner, sweet, for you.

Desdemona   Shall't be tonight, at supper?

Iago   [*to* **Othello**] Hm. I don't like that . . .

Othello   What did you say?

Iago   Oh, nothing, my lord. Or if . . . I really don't know . . .

Othello   Wasn't that Cassio leaving my wife?

Iago   Cassio, my lord? No, surely not. He wouldn't sneak away so guiltily on seeing you coming.

Othello   I'm sure it was him.

Desdemona   Greetings, my lord. I have been talking with a suitor here. A man who's not in your good books.

Othello   Who do you mean?

Desdemona   Why, your Lieutenant, Cassio. Good my lord, if I have any influence or ability to persuade you, make up with him immediately. If he doesn't truly love you – if he hasn't erred through ignorance rather than deliberately – then I'm no judge of an honest face. Please, call him back!

Othello   Did he go just now?

Desdemona   Yes indeed. So chastened that he left part of his grief with me, to suffer with him. Good love, call him back.

Othello   Not now, sweet Desdemona. Some other time.

Desdemona   Will that be soon?

Othello   The sooner, sweet, for your asking.

Desdemona   Shall it be tonight, at supper?

65 **Othello**   No, not tonight.

Desdemona   Tomorrow dinner then?

Othello   I shall not dine at home.
    I meet the captains at the citadel.

Desdemona   Why, then, tomorrow night, or Tuesday
70   morn,
    On Tuesday noon, or night; on Wednesday morn.
    I prithee name the time, but let it not
    Exceed three days. In faith, he's penitent;
    And yet his trespass in our common reason –
75   Save that, they say, the wars must make example
    Out of their best – is not almost a fault
    To incur a private check. When shall he come?
    Tell me, Othello. I wonder in my soul
    What you would ask me that I should deny,
80   Or stand so mammering on? What? Michael Cassio,
    That came a-wooing with you? And so many a time –
    When I have spoke of you dispraisingly –
    Hath ta'en your part, to have so much to do
    To bring him in? By'r Lady, I could do much –

85 **Othello**   Prithee, no more. Let him come when he will.
    I will deny thee nothing.

Desdemona   Why, this is not a boon:
    'Tis as I should entreat you wear your gloves,
    Or feed on nourishing dishes, or keep you warm,
90   Or sue to you to do a peculiar profit
    To your own person. Nay, when I have a suit
    Wherein I mean to touch your love indeed
    It shall be full of poise and difficulty
    And fearful to be granted.

Othello   No, not tonight.

Desdemona   Tomorrow at dinner, then?

Othello   I won't be dining at home. I'm meeting the captains at the citadel.

Desdemona   Well then: tomorrow night, or Tuesday morning, or Tuesday noon, or night; on Wednesday morning . . . Please, name the time, but not beyond three days. Really, he's very penitent. And his fault by normal standards – except in wartime when, they say, examples must be made of the best men – is hardly one to incur a personal rebuke. When shall he come? Tell me, Othello. What, I wonder, could you ask of me that I'd deny, or that I'd dither over? What? The Michael Cassio who came courting with you? Who so often took your part when I spoke disparagingly of you? To have to work so hard to have him reinstated? By all that's holy, I could do much –

Othello   Please, no more. Let him come when he wants to. I will deny you nothing.

Desdemona   Why, this is no favour! It's as if I should beg you to wear your gloves, or eat nourishing food, or keep yourself warm, or do yourself some personal good. No: when I have a request that's really intended to test your love, it will be extremely delicate and difficult, and worrying to grant!

95 **Othello**   I will deny thee nothing.
   Whereon, I do beseech thee, grant me this:
   To leave me but a little to myself.

Desdemona   Shall I deny you? No; farewell, my lord.

Othello   Farewell, my Desdemona. I'll come to thee
100   straight.

Desdemona   Emilia, come. Be as your fancies teach you.
   Whate'er you be, I am obedient.

                    [*Exeunt* **Desdemona** *and* **Emilia**]

Othello   Excellent wretch! Perdition catch my soul
   But I do love thee! And when I love thee not,
105   Chaos is come again.

Iago   My noble lord –

Othello   What dost thou say, Iago?

Iago   Did Michael Cassio,
   When you wooed my lady, know of your love?

110 **Othello**   He did, from first to last. Why dost thou ask?

Iago   But for a satisfaction of my thought –
   No further harm.

Othello   Why of thy thought, Iago?

Iago   I did not think he had been acquainted with her.

115 **Othello**   Oh yes, and went between us very often.

Iago   Indeed?

Othello   Indeed? Ay, indeed. Discern'st thou aught in
      that?
   Is he not honest?

120 **Iago**   Honest, my lord?

Othello I will deny you nothing. With that, I beg you, grant me this: leave me to myself for a while.

Desdemona Shall I deny you? No! Farewell, my lord.

Othello Farewell, my Desdemona. I'll be with you soon.

Desdemona Emilia, come. [*To* **Othello**] Do what you wish. Whatever that may be, I'll fall in with you.

[**Desdemona** *and* **Emilia** *leave*]

Othello The little rogue! The devil take my soul, but I adore you! Should I not, my world would end!

Iago My noble lord.

Othello Yes, Iago?

Iago Did Michael Cassio, when you wooed your wife, know of your love?

Othello He did. From first to last. Why do you ask?

Iago Just to confirm something I was thinking. Nothing worse.

Othello What were you thinking, Iago?

Iago I didn't realise he knew her.

Othello Oh yes, and he carried messages between us very often.

Iago Indeed!

Othello Indeed? Yes, indeed. Is there something you detect in that? Isn't he an honest man?

Iago Honest, my lord?

Othello   Honest? Ay, honest.

Iago   My lord, for aught I know.

Othello   What dost thou think?

Iago   Think, my lord?

125 **Othello**   'Think, my lord'! By heaven, he echoes me,
As if there were some monster in his thought
Too hideous to be shown. Thou dost mean something.
I heard thee say but now, thou lik'st not that,
When Cassio left my wife. What didst not like?
130   And when I told thee he was of my counsel
In my whole course of wooing, thou cried'st 'Indeed!'
And didst contract and purse thy brow together,
As if thou then hadst shut up in thy brain
Some horrible conceit. If thou dost love me,
135   Show me thy thought.

Iago   My lord, you know I love you.

Othello   I think thou dost;
And for I know thou art full of love and honesty,
And weighest thy words before thou giv'st them breath,
140   Therefore these stops of thine affright me more:
For such things in a false disloyal knave
Are tricks of custom; but in a man that's just,
They're close denotements, working from the heart,
That passion cannot rule.

145 **Iago**   For Michael Cassio,
I dare be sworn I think that he is honest.

Othello   I think so too.

Iago   Men should be what they seem;
Or those that be not, would they might seem none!

Othello   Honest? Yes – honest.

Iago   My lord. For all I know . . .

Othello   What do you think?

Iago   Think, my lord?

Othello   'Think, my lord'! By heaven, he echoes me as if there were some monster in his thoughts too hideous to be shown. You mean something. I heard you say just now 'I don't like that', when Cassio left my wife. What didn't you like? And when I told you he was in my confidence throughout my courtship, you cried 'Indeed!' and furrowed your brow as though you had some horrible idea in your head. If you love me, tell me what is on your mind.

Iago   My lord, you know I love you.

Othello   I think you do. And because I know you are full of love and honesty, and that you weigh your words before you speak, these pauses of yours frighten me all the more. Such things are the standard tricks of a false, disloyal rogue: but in a man of integrity, they are instinctive reactions coming from the heart, which feelings cannot control.

Iago   As for Michael Cassio, I think he's honest . . .

Othello   I think so too.

Iago   Men ought to be what they seem to be; the false ones should look different.

150 **Othello**   Certain, men should be what they seem.

Iago   Why, then, I think Cassio's an honest man.

Othello   Nay, yet there's more in this.
I prithee speak to me as to thy thinkings,
As thou dost ruminate, and give thy worst of thoughts
155   The worst of words.

Iago   Good my lord, pardon me;
Though I am bound to every act of duty,
I am not bound to that all slaves are free to:
Utter my thoughts. Why, say they are vile and false?
160   As where's that palace whereinto foul things
Sometimes intrude not? Who has a breast so pure,
But some uncleanly apprehensions
Keep leets and law-days, and in session sit
With meditations lawful?

165 **Othello**   Thou dost conspire against thy friend, Iago,
If thou but think'st him wronged, and makest his ear
A stranger to thy thoughts.

Iago   I do beseech you,
Though I perchance am vicious in my guess –
170   As I confess it is my nature's plague
To spy into abuses, and oft my jealousy
Shapes faults that are not – that your wisdom then,
From one that so imperfectly conjects,
Would take no notice, nor build yourself a trouble
175   Out of my scattering and unsure observance.
It were not for your quiet nor your good,
Nor for my manhood, honesty, or wisdom,
To let you know my thoughts.

Othello   What dost thou mean?

Othello   Certainly, men should be what they seem.

Iago   Well, then, I think Cassio's an honest man . . .

Othello   No; there's something more in this. I want you to share your thoughts with me, and call a spade a spade, no matter what.

Iago   Good my lord, forgive me. Though I am bound to carry out all my duties, I am not obliged speak my thoughts, which is a freedom given to slaves. Why, suppose they are vile, and untrue? Where is the palace that's exempt from foul intruders? Who is so perfect that there are not times when improper thoughts sit side-by-side with decent ones?

Othello   You are conspiring against your friend, Iago, if you believe he's being wronged, but don't tell him what you are thinking.

Iago   With respect, since I could be guessing incorrectly – I confess I have a chronic tendency to spy out misconduct, and often my suspicious nature sees faults which are not there – I would ask you in your wisdom to disregard a man like me who's often wrong, and not distress yourself on account of my haphazard observations. It would be good neither for your peace of mind and your welfare, nor my integrity, honesty and common-sense, to let you know my thoughts.

Othello   What do you mean?

180 **Iago**   Good name in man and woman, dear my lord,
Is the immediate jewel of their souls.
Who steals my purse, steals trash; 'tis something,
    nothing;
'Twas mine, 'tis his, and has been slave to thousands:
185 But he that filches from me my good name
Robs me of that which not enriches him
And makes me poor indeed.

Othello   By heaven, I'll know thy thoughts.

Iago   You cannot, if my heart were in your hand,
190 Nor shall not, whilst 'tis in my custody.
Oh, beware, my lord, of jealousy!
It is the green-eyed monster, which doth mock
The meat it feeds on. That cuckold lives in bliss
Who certain of his fate loves not his wronger;
195 But oh, what damned minutes tells he o'er,
Who dotes, yet doubts, suspects, yet strongly loves!

Othello   Oh misery!

Iago   Poor and content is rich, and rich enough;
But riches fineless is as poor as winter,
200 To him that ever fears he shall be poor.
Good God, the souls of all my tribe defend
From jealousy!

Othello   Why, why is this?
Think'st thou I'd make a life of jealousy,
205 To follow still the changes of the moon
With fresh suspicions? No, to be once in doubt
Is once to be resolved. Exchange me for a goat,
When I shall turn the business of my soul
To such exsufflicate and blown surmises,
210 Matching thy inference. 'Tis not to make me jealous

Iago   A man or woman's good name, my dear lord, is the most precious jewel of their souls. Whoever steals my money, steals trash. It's something, but nothing of great value. It was mine, now it's his. It's been at the service of thousands. But the man who steals my good name robs me of something that gains him nothing, and makes me very poor.

Othello   By heaven, I'll know your thoughts!

Iago   You cannot, even if my heart were in your hand; nor will you, while it's in my custody. Oh, beware of jealousy, my lord. It is a green-eyed monster that mocks the meat it feeds on. Blissful the man with the unfaithful wife, who knows the worst and hates the culprit. But oh, how prolonged is the torment of the man who's infatuated but insecure, who suspects yet continues to adore!

Othello   What misery!

Iago   To be poor and happy is to be rich, and rich enough. But infinite wealth is abject poverty to the man in constant fear of being poor. Good God, may the souls of all my ancestors defend me against jealousy!

Othello   Why do you say all this? Do you think I'd lead a life of jealousy, with fresh suspicions for every new phase of the moon? No. To be once in doubt is to be once resolved. Say I'm a randy goat if ever I'm obsessed with bloated, fly-blown suspicions such as you are on about. It doesn't

To say my wife is fair, loves company,
Is free of speech, sings, plays, and dances well:
Where virtue is, these are more virtuous.
Nor from mine own weak merits will I draw
215   The smallest fear or doubt of her revolt,
For she had eyes and chose me. No, Iago,
I'll see before I doubt; when I doubt, prove;
And on the proof, there is no more but this:
Away at once with love or jealousy!

220   **Iago**   I am glad of it: for now I shall have reason
To show the love and duty that I bear you
With franker spirit. Therefore, as I am bound,
Receive it from me. I speak not yet of proof.
Look to your wife; observe her well with Cassio;
225   Wear your eye thus: not jealous, nor secure.
I would not have your free and noble nature,
Out of self-bounty, be abused. Look to't.
I know our country disposition well;
In Venice they do let God see the pranks
230   They dare not show their husbands; their best conscience
Is not to leave undone, but keep unknown.

Othello   Dost thou say so?

Iago   She did deceive her father, marrying you,
And when she seemed to shake, and fear your looks,
235   She loved them most.

Othello   And so she did.

Iago   Why, go to, then!
She that so young could give out such a seeming,
To seal her father's eyes up close as oak –
240   He thought 'twas witchcraft – But I am much to blame;
I humbly do beseech you of your pardon
For too much loving you.

make me jealous to say my wife is beautiful, loves
company, is talkative, sings, plays music, and
dances well. These are added virtues of the
virtuous. Neither will I entertain the smallest fear or
suspicion of her unfaithfulness because of my own
shortcomings. She had eyes, and she chose me. No,
Iago. I'll see for myself before I suspect. When I
suspect, I'll want proof. Once proved there's only
one thing left – immediately to do away with love,
or do away with jealousy!

Iago   Good. Now I am justified in showing the love
and loyalty I have for you more openly. Therefore
take note of what I am obliged to say. I do not, as
yet, speak of proof. Keep an eye on your wife.
Watch her carefully when she's with Cassio.
Observe her thus: neither jealously, nor
complacently. I would not have your open and
noble nature abused. So watch out. I know our
promiscuous inclinations well: in Venice, God alone
knows what pranks wives are up to which they dare
not tell their husbands. Their morality is based not
on abstention, but on keeping things dark.

Othello   Really?

Iago   She deceived her father when she married you.
And when she seemed to tremble and fear your
looks, she loved them most.

Othello   And so she did.

Iago   Well, I mean! So young a woman to be so
deceitful! To blind her father's eyes so utterly – he
thought it was witchcraft! But this is wrong of me. I
humbly beg your pardon for loving you too much.

Othello   I am bound to thee for ever.

Iago   I see this hath a little dashed your spirits.

245 **Othello**   Not a jot, not a jot.

Iago   In faith, I fear it has.
I hope you will consider what is spoke
Comes from my love; but I do see you are moved.
I am to pray you, not to strain my speech
250 To grosser issues, nor to larger reach
Than to suspicion.

Othello   I will not.

Iago   Should you do so, my lord,
My speech should fall into such vile success
255 Which my thoughts aim not at. Cassio's my trusty
friend.
My lord, I see you are moved.

Othello   No, not much moved.
I do not think but Desdemona's honest.

260 **Iago**   Long live she so! And long live you to think so!

Othello   And yet, how nature erring from itself –

Iago   Ay, there's the point: as, to be bold with you,
Not to affect many proposed matches
Of her own clime, complexion, and degree,
265 Whereto we see in all things nature tends;
Fie! One may smell in such a will most rank,
Foul disproportion; thoughts unnatural.
But, pardon me; I do not in position
Distinctly speak of her, though I may fear
270 Her will, recoiling to her better judgement,
May fall to match you with her country forms,
And happily repent.

Othello   I am eternally indebted to you.

Iago   I see this has somewhat depressed you . . .

Othello   Not a bit, not a bit . . .

Iago   Really, I think it has. I hope you will consider what I've said as coming from my love. But I can see you are upset. For heaven's sake do not interpret my words too grossly, nor regard them as more than suspicion.

Othello   I won't.

Iago   Should you do so, my lord, my words would have a worse effect than I intended. Cassio's my good friend . . . My lord, you *are* upset.

Othello   No, not very. I'm sure Desdemona is chaste.

Iago   Long may she be so! And long live you to think so!

Othello   And yet, how nature can go astray —

Iago   Yes, that's the point! As, for example — to be perfectly frank with you — her rejecting many proposed marriages to men of her own country, colour and rank, which is nature's way in everything. Pah! One detects in such an instinct a corrupt and foul unseemliness: perverted thinking! But forgive me. I cannot say this of her for certain, but I fear that when her better judgement prevails over her desire, she may compare you with her fellow-countrymen and possibly repent.

Othello   Farewell, farewell.
If more thou dost perceive, let me know more.
275   Set on thy wife to observe. Leave me, Iago.

Iago   [*going*] My lord, I take my leave.

Othello   Why did I marry? This honest creature doubtless
Sees and knows more, much more than he unfolds.

Iago   [*returning*] My lord, I would I might entreat your
280   honour
To scan this thing no further. Leave it to time:
Though it be fit that Cassio have his place –
For sure he fills it up with great ability –
Yet, if you please to hold him off awhile,
285   You shall by that perceive him and his means;
Note if your lady strain her entertainment
With any strong or vehement importunity;
Much will be seen in that. In the meantime,
Let me be thought too busy in my fears,
290   As worthy cause I have to fear I am,
And hold her free, I do beseech your honour.

Othello   Fear not my government.

Iago   I once more take my leave.

                                                    [*Exit*]

Othello   This fellow's of exceeding honesty,
295   And knows all qualities with a learned spirit
Of human dealings. If I do prove her haggard,
Though that her jesses were my dear heart-strings,
I'd whistle her off, and let her down the wind
To prey at fortune. Haply, for I am black
300   And have not those soft parts of conversation
That chamberers have; or for I am declined
Into the vale of years – yet that's not much –

Othello   Farewell, farewell. If you notice anything else, tell me more. Get your wife to watch her. Leave me, Iago.

Iago   My lord, I'll say goodbye. [*He starts to leave*]

Othello   Why did I marry? This honest fellow doubtless sees and knows more, much more, than he's prepared to tell.

Iago   [*returning*] My lord, could I suggest that you think no more about this matter? Leave it to time. Though it's right that Cassio should have his job again – undoubtedly, he's very able – nevertheless, if you should keep him waiting a little longer, you'll be able to watch him and his tactics. Note if your lady-wife nags persistently and vehemently to have him reinstated. That will tell you a great deal. In the meantime, take it I'm being over-cautious, as I've good reason to suppose I am. Give her the benefit of the doubt, I beg you.

Othello   I'll be sensible, don't worry.

Iago   I'll say goodbye again.

[*He bows and leaves*]

Othello   This fellow's exceedingly honest and very worldly-wise. If I found she was like an untameable wild hawk, I'd free her to fend for herself even though my own dear heart-strings held her. Perhaps she's gone because I'm black, and lack the smooth talk that ladies' men have; or because I'm getting on in years – though not all that much. I've been

She's gone: I am abused, and my relief
Must be to loathe her. Oh, curse of marriage!
305   That we can call these delicate creatures ours
And not their appetites! I had rather be a toad
And live upon the vapour of a dungeon
Than keep a corner in the thing I love
For others' uses. Yet 'tis the plague of great ones;
310   Prerogatived are they less than the base.
'Tis destiny unshunnable, like death:
Even then this forked plague is fated to us
When we do quicken. Desdemona comes:
If she be false, oh, then heaven mocks itself!
315   I'll not believe it.

[*Enter* **Desdemona** *and* **Emilia**]

Desdemona   How now, my dear Othello!
Your dinner, and the generous islanders
By you invited, do attend your presence.

Othello   I am to blame.

320   **Desdemona**   Why do you speak so faintly?
Are you not well?

Othello   I have a pain upon my forehead, here.

Desdemona   Faith, that's with watching: 'twill away
again.
325   Let me but bind your head, within this hour
It will be well.

Othello   Your napkin is too little.

[*She drops her handkerchief*]

Let it alone. Come, I'll go in with you.

Desdemona   I am very sorry that you are not well.

[*Exeunt* **Othello** *and* **Desdemona**]

deceived, and my only relief is to loathe her. Oh, the curse of marriage! That we can call these dainty creatures ours, but not their lusts! I'd rather be a toad, and live on the stench of a dungeon, than keep a part of the one I love for the use of others. Yet, it's the plague of the great. They are less privileged than the humble. It's an inescapable fate, like death: we are fated from birth to be deceived by women. Here's Desdemona now.

[**Desdemona** *enters with* **Emilia**]

If she's unfaithful, heaven mocks its own likeness! I won't believe it!

Desdemona   Greetings, my dear Othello! Your dinner, and your guests the noble islanders, are waiting for you.

Othello   I am to blame.

Desdemona   Why do you speak so softly? Aren't you well?

Othello   I have a headache.

Desdemona   Now that's with getting too little sleep. It will go. Let me tie a handkerchief tightly round your forehead, and it will be better within the hour.

Othello   It's too small.

[*He brushes it aside and it drops to the ground*]

Let it be. Come, I'll go in with you.

Desdemona   I'm sorry you're not well.

[**Othello** *and* **Desdemona** *leave*]

330 **Emilia**   I am glad I have found this napkin;
          This was her first remembrance from the Moor.
          My wayward husband hath a hundred times
          Wooed me to steal it; but she so loves the token –
          For he conjured her she should ever keep it –
335   That she reserves it evermore about her
          To kiss and talk to. I'll have the work taken out,
          And give't Iago.
          What he will do with it, Heaven knows, not I;
          I nothing, but to please his fantasy.

          [*Enter* **Iago**]

340 **Iago**   How now? What do you here alone?

      Emilia   Do not you chide: I have a thing for you.

      Iago   A thing for me? It is a common thing –

      Emilia   Ha!

      Iago   To have a foolish wife.

345 **Emilia**   Oh, is that all? What will you give me now
          For that same handkerchief?

      Iago   What handkerchief?

      Emilia   What handkerchief!
          Why that the Moor first gave to Desdemona;
350   That which so often you did bid me steal.

      Iago   Hast stolen it from her?

      Emilia   No faith, she let it drop by negligence,
          And to the advantage, I, being here, took't up.
          Look, here it is.

355 **Iago**   A good wench! Give it to me.

Emilia   [*picking the handkerchief up*] I'm glad I've found this handkerchief. It was the first present the Moor ever gave her. My devious husband has begged me to steal it a hundred times. But she loves the gift so much – he entreated her to keep it forever – that she always has it with her, to kiss and talk to. I'll have it copied and give it to Iago. What he will do with it, heaven knows, not me. I only want to satisfy his whim.

[**Iago** *enters*]

Iago   Well? What are you doing here alone?

Emilia   Don't scold. I've got something for you.

Iago   Some 'thing' for me? [*He leers at her*] It's a vulgar thing –

Emilia   [*detecting an obscenity*] Now then!

Iago   [*dodging it*] . . . to have a foolish wife!

Emilia   [*realizing she's been tricked*] Oh, is that all? [*Her manner changes*] What will you give me now for that handkerchief?

Iago   What handkerchief?

Emilia   What handkerchief! Why, the one the Moor gave to Desdemona as his first present: the one which you so often asked me to steal.

Iago   Have you stolen it from her?

Emilia   No, indeed! She let it drop by accident. Having the luck to be here, I picked it up.

Iago   Good girl! Give it me.

Emilia   What will you do with it, that you have been so earnest
To have me filch it?

Iago   [*snatching it*] Why, what is that to you?

360 **Emilia**   If it be not for some purpose of import,
Give't me again. Poor lady, she'll run mad
When she shall lack it.

Iago   Be not you known on't; I have use for it.
Go, leave me.

[*Exit* **Emilia**]

365   I will in Cassio's lodging lose this napkin,
And let him find it. Trifles light as air
Are to the jealous confirmations strong
As proofs of holy writ. This may do something.
The Moor already changes with my poison.
370   Dangerous conceits are in their natures poisons,
Which at the first are scarce found to distaste,
But with a little act upon the blood,
Burn like the mines of sulphur. I did say so.

[*Enter* **Othello**]

Look where he comes! Not poppy, nor mandragora,
375   Nor all the drowsy syrups of the world,
Shall ever medicine thee to that sweet sleep
Which thou owed'st yesterday.

Othello   Ha, ha, false to me?

Iago   Why, how now, General? No more of that.

380 **Othello**   Avaunt, be gone! Thou hast set me on the rack.
I swear 'tis better to be much abused,
Than but to know't a little.

Emilia   What do you intend to do with it, that you've been so anxious to have me steal it?

Iago   [*snatching it*] Why, what's that to you?

Emilia   If it's not for some important purpose, give it back to me. Poor lady, she'll go mad when she misses it.

Iago   I've got a use for it. Go, leave me. It's best you do not know.

[**Emilia** *goes*]

I'll place this handkerchief in Cassio's lodgings, so he'll find it. To the jealous, trivial things are proofs as strong as holy writ. This might do something. The Moor is already a different man as a result of my poisonous words. Fertile imaginations are poisons in themselves: at first they don't seem bad, but given time to act upon the blood, they burn like sulphur mines. So say I.

[**Othello** *enters*]

Look, here he comes! Neither opium, nor mandragora, nor all the tranquilizing drugs on earth, will ever induce the sweet sleep you enjoyed in days gone by!

Othello   False to me!

Iago   Why, greetings, General! You mustn't talk like that!

Othello   Away! Begone! You have put me on the rack. I swear it's better to be deceived outright than nagged by doubts.

Iago   How now, my lord!

Othello   What sense had I of her stolen hours of lust?
385   I saw't not, thought it not, it harmed not me.
    I slept the next night well, was free and merry;
    I found not Cassio's kisses on her lips.
    He that is robbed, not wanting what is stolen,
    Let him not know't, and he's not robbed at all.

390 **Iago**   I am sorry to hear this.

Othello   I had been happy if the general camp,
    Pioners and all, had tasted her sweet body,
    So I had nothing known. Oh, now, for ever
    Farewell the tranquil mind! Farewell content!
395   Farewell the plumed troops and the big wars
    That make ambition virtue – Oh, farewell!
    Farewell the neighing steed, and the shrill trump,
    The spirit-stirring drum, the ear-piercing fife,
    The royal banner and all quality,
400   Pride, pomp and circumstance of glorious war!
    And, oh you mortal engines, whose rude throats
    The immortal Jove's dread clamours counterfeit,
    Farewell! Othello's occupation's gone.

Iago   Is't possible, my lord?

405 **Othello**   Villain, be sure thou prove my love a whore;
    Be sure of it: give me the ocular proof,
    Or by the worth of mine eternal soul,
    Thou hadst been better have been born a dog
    Than answer my waked wrath!

410 **Iago**   Is't come to this?

Othello   Make me to see't: or, at the least, so prove it
    That the probation bear no hinge nor loop
    To hang a doubt on: or woe upon thy life!

Iago   Come, my lord!

Othello   What did I know of her stolen hours of lust? I didn't see anything; think anything; it did me no harm. I slept the next night contentedly. I was carefree and merry. I found none of Cassio's kisses on her lips. The man who is robbed and doesn't want what is stolen isn't robbed at all if he knows nothing of the theft.

Iago   I'm sorry to hear this.

Othello   I'd have been happy if the entire camp, trench-diggers and all, had tasted her sweet body, provided I knew nothing! Farewell forever to a tranquil mind! Farewell contentment! Farewell the spectacular troops, and the big wars that make a virtue of ambition. Oh, farewell! Farewell the neighing horse, and the shrill trumpet, the spirit-stirring drum, the ear-piercing fife, the royal banner, and all the pride, pomp and ceremony of glorious war! And oh, you lethal cannon, whose muzzles imitate the sound of thunder, farewell! Othello has no occupation now.

Iago   How can that be, my lord?

Othello   Villain, be sure you can prove my beloved is a whore! Be sure of it! Prove it to my own eyes, or upon my precious and eternal soul you had been better born a dog than suffer my vengeance!

Iago   Is this real?

Othello   Fix it so that I see it. Or at least, so prove it that the evidence is foolproof – or you're as good as dead!

Iago   My noble lord –

415 **Othello**   If thou dost slander her and torture me,
Never pray more; abandon all remorse;
On horror's head horrors accumulate;
Do deeds to make heaven weep, all earth amazed:
For nothing canst thou to damnation add
420 Greater than that.

Iago   Oh grace! Oh heaven defend me!
Are you a man? Have you a soul? Or sense?
God bu'y you. Take mine office. Oh wretched fool,
That lov'st to make thine honesty a vice!
425 Oh monstrous world! Take note, take note, oh world!
To be direct and honest is not safe.
I thank you for this profit, and from hence
I'll love no friend, since love breeds such offence.

Othello   Nay, stay: thou shouldst be honest.

430 **Iago**   I should be wise; for honesty's a fool
And loses that it works for.

Othello   By the world,
I think my wife be honest, and think she is not;
I think that thou art just, and think thou art not.
435 I'll have some proof. Her name that was as fresh
As Dian's visage is now begrimed and black
As mine own face. If there be cords or knives,
Poison or fire or suffocating streams,
I'll not endure it. Would I were satisfied!

440 **Iago**   I see, sir, you are eaten up with passion.
I do repent me that I put it to you.
You would be satisfied?

Othello   Would? Nay, I will!

Iago   My noble lord –

Othello   If you have slandered her and tortured me, never pray again. Abandon all pity; pile horror upon horror; do deeds to make the angels weep, and amaze the world: because you cannot add to your damnation a sin greater than that!

Iago   Oh, God! Oh, heaven defend me! Are you a man? Have you a soul? Or feeling? All right, then: strip me of my rank. Oh, wretched fool, for taking honesty to excess! Oh, monstrous world! Take note, take note, oh world! To be forthright and honest is not safe. I thank you for this lesson: from now on I'll not love a friend, since love breeds such offence!

[*He makes to go*]

Othello   No, stay. You should be honest.

Iago   I should be wise: honesty is idiotic, and destroys what it tries to achieve.

Othello   Assuredly, I think my wife is chaste, and think she isn't; I think that you are honourable, and think you aren't. I want proof! Her name, that was as fair as the face of Diana [*goddess of chastity*], is now begrimed, and as black as mine. I'll not endure it while there are ropes, or knives, or poison, or fire, or streams to drown in! If only I knew!

Iago   I see, sir, that you are consumed with passion. I'm sorry now that I spoke out. You want proof?

Othello   Want? No: I demand it!

Iago   And may. But how? How satisfied, my lord?
445   Would you, the supervisor, grossly gape on?
Behold her topped?

Othello   Death and damnation! Oh!

Iago   It were a tedious difficulty, I think,
To bring them to that prospect. Damn them then
450   If ever mortal eyes do see them bolster
More than their own! What then? How then?
What shall I say? Where's satisfaction?
It is impossible you should see this,
Were they as prime as goats, as hot as monkeys,
455   As salt as wolves in pride, and fools as gross
As ignorance made drunk. But yet, I say,
If imputation and strong circumstance,
Which lead directly to the door of truth,
Will give you satisfaction, you might have't.

460 **Othello**   Give me a living reason she's disloyal.

Iago   I do not like the office.
But sith I am entered in this cause so far –
Pricked to't by foolish honesty and love –
I will go on. I lay with Cassio lately,
465   And being troubled with a raging tooth
I could not sleep.
There are a kind of men so loose of soul
That in their sleeps will mutter their affairs;
One of this kind is Cassio.
470   In sleep I heard him say: 'Sweet Desdemona,
Let us be wary, let us hide our loves';
And then, sir, would he gripe and wring my hand,
Cry 'Oh sweet creature!' and then kiss me hard,
As if he plucked up kisses by the roots,
475   That grew upon my lips; then laid his leg
Over my thigh, and sighed and kissed, and then
Cried 'Cursed fate, that gave thee to the Moor!'

Iago   And may get it. But how? What proof, my lord? Would you, the voyeur, gawk at her lasciviously? Watch her being layed?

Othello   Death and damnation, oh!

Iago   It would be exceptionally difficult, I think, to fix that up. Bedamned if eyes other than their own ever see them share a pillow! What then? How then? What's the answer? Where's the proof? It's impossible for you to see them in the act, even if they were as lecherous as goats, as lusty as monkeys, as wanton as wolves on heat; and fools as stupid as intoxicated morons. But nevertheless, if strong circumstantial evidence leading directly to the truth will give you the proof you need, you might have it.

Othello   Give me convincing evidence that she's disloyal!

Iago   I don't like the task. But since I'm so involved, urged on by foolish honesty and love, I'll proceed. I slept with Cassio recently, and being troubled with raging toothache I couldn't sleep. There are some men so discreet that they talk about their affairs in their sleep. Cassio is one such. In his sleep I heard him say, 'Sweet Desdemona, let us be careful; let us keep our love secret'. And then, sir, he would grip my hand and wring it; cry 'Oh, sweet creature!' and then kiss me hard, as if he plucked kisses up by the roots that were growing on my lips. Then he laid his leg over my thigh, and sighed, and kissed, and then cried 'Curse the fate that gave you to the Moor!'

Othello   Oh monstrous! Monstrous!

Iago   Nay, this was but his dream.

480 **Othello**   But this denoted a foregone conclusion.

Iago   'Tis a shrewd doubt, though it be but a dream:
And this may help to thicken other proofs
That do demonstrate thinly.

Othello   I'll tear her all to pieces!

485 **Iago**   Nay, but be wise: yet we see nothing done,
She may be honest yet. Tell me but this:
Have you not sometimes seen a handkerchief,
Spotted with strawberries, in your wife's hand?

Othello   I gave her such a one; 'twas my first gift.

490 **Iago**   I know not that: but such a handkerchief –
I am sure it was your wife's – did I today
See Cassio wipe his beard with.

Othello   If it be that –

Iago   If it be that, or any that was hers,
495   It speaks against her with the other proofs.

Othello   Oh, that the slave had forty thousand lives!
One is too poor, too weak for my revenge.
Now do I see 'tis true. Look here, Iago –
All my fond love thus do I blow to heaven:
500   'Tis gone.
Arise, black vengeance, from thy hollow cell!
Yield up, oh love, thy crown and hearted throne
To tyrannous hate! Swell, bosom, with thy fraught,
For 'tis of aspics' tongues!

505 **Iago**   Pray be content.

Othello   Oh blood, Iago, blood!

Othello   Oh, monstrous, monstrous!

Iago   Yes, but this was only a dream . . .

Othello   It indicates adultery in the past!

Iago   A reasonable inference, even if it was only a dream. And it may help to confirm other evidence that's only flimsy.

Othello   I'll tear her into little pieces!

Iago   Easy now: we have no visual evidence yet. She could still be innocent. Just tell me this: haven't you sometimes seen a handkerchief embroidered with strawberries in your wife's hand?

Othello   I gave her one like that. It was my first gift.

Iago   I wouldn't know about that, but today I saw Cassio wipe his beard with such a handkerchief: I'm sure it was your wife's . . .

Othello   If it's the same . . .

Iago   If it's the same, or any of hers, it adds to the proof against her.

Othello   Oh, I wish the wretch had forty thousand lives! One is not enough, too inadequate, for my revenge. Now I see it's true. Look here, Iago, all my fond love I blow into the air like this [*he demonstrates*]. It's gone. Black vengeance, come from your deep cave! Love, surrender to pitiless hate your crown and throne that's fixed within the heart! And heart, swell with your burden: it's made of venomous snakes!

Iago   Control yourself.

Othello   Oh blood, Iago, blood!

Iago   Patience, I say. Your mind perhaps may change.

Othello   Never, Iago. Like to the Pontic sea,
Whose icy current and compulsive course
510 Ne'er feels retiring ebb, but keeps due on
To the Propontic and the Hellespont,
Even so my bloody thoughts with violent pace
Shall ne'er look back, ne'er ebb to humble love,
Till that a capable and wide revenge
515 Swallow them up. Now, by yond marble heaven:
In the due reverence of a sacred vow
I here engage my words.

[*He kneels*]

Iago   Do not rise yet.

[*He kneels*]

Witness you ever-burning lights above,
520 You elements, that clip us round about,
Witness that here Iago doth give up
The execution of his wit, hands, heart,
To wronged Othello's service. Let him command,
And to obey shall be in me remorse,
525 What bloody business ever.

[*They rise*]

Othello   I greet thy love,
Not with vain thanks, but with acceptance bounteous;
And will upon the instant put thee to't.
Within these three days let me hear thee say
530 That Cassio's not alive.

Iago   My friend is dead;
'Tis done at your request. But let her live.

Iago   Be patient, I say. Perhaps you'll change your mind.

Othello   Never, Iago. Just like the Black Sea, whose cold waters and steady flow never faulter, but which keeps right on to the Sea of Marmora and the Dardanelles, my fast-racing murderous thoughts will never look back, never subside into humble love, till they are consumed in abundant and total revenge. Now, by heaven's grandeur, with the solemn reverence of a sacred vow, I here pledge my word!

[*He kneels in prayer*]

Iago   Do not rise yet.

[*He kneels at* **Othello's** *side*]

Witness, you stars; you elements that encompass us; witness that here, Iago dedicates his mind, his hands, his heart to the service of the wronged Othello. Let him command, and to obey will be my moral duty, even if it means shedding blood.

[*They rise*]

Othello   I acknowledge your love, not with vain thanks, but with warm-hearted acceptance, and I will put you to the proof immediately. By three days at the latest, let me hear you say that Cassio is not alive.

Iago   My friend is dead. It's done, at your request. But let her live.

Othello   Damn her, lewd minx! Oh, damn her, damn her!
Come go with me apart. I will withdraw
535   To furnish me with some swift means of death
For the fair devil. Now art thou my Lieutenant.

Iago   I am your own for ever.

[Exeunt]

Scene 4

Cyprus. Before the Castle. Enter **Desdemona, Emilia,** *and*
Clown.

Desdemona   Do you know, sirrah, where Lieutenant
Cassio lies?

Clown   I dare not say he lies anywhere.

Desdemona   Why, man?

5   **Clown**   He's a soldier, and for one to say a soldier lies is
stabbing.

Desdemona   Go to! Where lodges he?

Clown   To tell you where he lodges is to tell you where I
lie.

10   **Desdemona**   Can anything be made of this?

Clown   I know not where he lodges, and for me to devise a
lodging, and say he lies here, or he lies there, were to lie
in mine own throat.

Desdemona   Can you inquire him out, and be edified by
15   report?

Othello   Damn her, the lewd minx! Oh, damn her, damn her! Let's go our separate ways. I'll go to my room to equip myself with some swift means of death for the beautiful devil! You are my Lieutenant now.

Iago   Your faithful servant, evermore.

[*They go*]

Scene 4

Desdemona, Emilia *and the* **Clown** *enter.*

Desdemona   Fellow, do you know where Lieutenant Cassio lies?

Clown   I daren't say that he lies anywhere.

Desdemona   Why, man?

Clown   He's a soldier, and to say a soldier tells lies is offensive.

Desdemona   Away with you! Where does he lodge?

Clown   To tell you where he lodges is to tell you where I lie.

Desdemona   How do you mean?

Clown   I don't know where he lodges; and for me to invent a lodging, and say he lies here, or lies there, would be to tell a great big fib.

Desdemona   Can you ask around for him? And learn something from what you're told?

Clown   I will catechize the world for him, that is, make
questions, and by them answer.

Desdemona   Seek him; bid him come hither; tell him I
have moved my lord on his behalf, and hope all will be
20   well.

Clown   To do this is within the compass of man's wit, and
therefore I will attempt the doing of it.

[*Exit*]

Desdemona   Where should I lose that handkerchief,
Emilia?

25   **Emilia**   I know not, madam.

Desdemona   Believe me, I had rather have lost my purse
Full of crusadoes; and, but my noble Moor
Is true of mind, and made of no such baseness
As jealous creatures are, it were enough
30   To put him to ill-thinking.

Emilia   Is he not jealous?

Desdemona   Who, he? I think the sun where he was born
Drew all such humours from him.

Emilia   Look where he comes.

[*Enter* **Othello**]

35   **Desdemona**   I will not leave him now. Let Cassio
Be called to him. How is't with you, my lord?

Othello   Well, my good lady. [*Aside*] Oh, hardness to
dissemble!
How do you, Desdemona?

40   **Desdemona**   Well, my good lord.

Othello   Give me your hand. This hand is moist, my lady.

172

Clown   I will catechize the world for him. In other
words, I'll put the questions, and answer them
myself.

Desdemona   Find him. Tell him to come here. Tell
him I've persuaded my husband on his behalf, and
hope all will be well.

Clown   To do this is within man's brain-power.
Therefore, I will attempt the doing of it.

[*He goes*]

Desdemona   Wherever did I lose that handkerchief,
Emilia?

Emilia   I don't know, madam.

Desdemona   Believe me, I'd rather have lost a
purseful of gold coins. But that my noble husband
the Moor is pure-thinking, and devoid of jealousy, it
would be enough to make him suspicious.

Emilia   Isn't he a jealous man?

Desdemona   Who? Othello? I think where he was
born, the sun scorched jealousy out of him!

Emilia   Here he is.

[**Othello** *enters*]

Desdemona   I won't leave him now. Call Cassio. How
are you, my lord?

Othello   Well, my good lady. [*Aside*] Oh, how hard it
is to pretend! [*Aloud*] How are you, Desdemona?

Desdemona   Well, my good lord.

Othello   Give me your hand. This hand is moist, my
lady.

Desdemona   It yet has felt no age, nor known no sorrow.

Othello   This argues fruitfulness and liberal heart.
Hot, hot and moist. This hand of yours requires
45   A sequester from liberty, fasting and praying,
Much castigation, exercise devout;
For there's a young and sweating devil here
That commonly rebels. 'Tis a good hand,
A frank one.

50   **Desdemona**   You may, indeed, say so:
For 'twas that hand that gave away my heart.

Othello   A liberal hand! The hearts of old gave hands;
But our new heraldry is hands, not hearts.

Desdemona   I cannot speak of this. Come now, your
55   promise.

Othello   What promise, chuck?

Desdemona   I have sent to bid Cassio come speak with
you.

Othello   I have a salt and sullen rheum offends me:
60   Lend me thy handkerchief.

Desdemona   Here, my lord.

Othello   That which I gave you.

Desdemona   I have it not about me.

Othello   Not?

65   **Desdemona**   No, faith, my lord.

Desdemona   So far it has known neither age nor sorrow.

Othello   This indicates amorousness and loose morals. Hot . . . Hot and moist . . . This hand of yours implies a need for restraint, fasting and prayer; a great deal of self-control, and solemn worship; because there's a young and sweating devil here that frequently breaks out. It's a good hand. A generous one.

Desdemona   Well said. It was that hand that gave away my heart.

Othello   A liberal hand! In the old days, hearts and hands went together. Nowadays handshakes can't be trusted.

Desdemona   I wouldn't know. Come now. Your promise!

Othello   What promise, chick?

Desdemona   I've asked Cassio to come and speak to you.

Othello   I'm troubled with a runny nose – lend me your handkerchief.

Desdemona   Here, my lord.

Othello   The one I gave you.

Desdemona   I haven't got it with me.

Othello   You haven't?

Desdemona   No, really my lord.

Othello   That is a fault. That handkerchief
Did an Egyptian to my mother give;
She was a charmer and could almost read
The thoughts of people. She told her, while she kept it,
70   'Twould make her amiable and subdue my father
Entirely to her love; but, if she lost it
Or made a gift of it, my father's eye
Should hold her loathed, and his spirits should hunt
After new fancies. She, dying, gave it me,
75   And bid me, when my fate would have me wive,
To give it her. I did so; and take heed on't:
Make it a darling, like your precious eye.
To lose or give't away were such perdition
As nothing else could match.

80 **Desdemona**   Is't possible?

Othello   'Tis true: there's magic in the web of it.
A sibyl, that had numbered in the world
The sun to make two hundred compasses,
In her prophetic fury sewed the work:
85   The worms were hallowed that did breed the silk.
And it was dyed in mummy, which the skilful
Conserved of maidens' hearts.

Desdemona   Indeed! Is't true?

Othello   Most veritable; therefore look to't well.

90 **Desdemona**   Then would to God that I had never seen it!

Othello   Ha! Wherefore?

Desdemona   Why do you speak so startingly and rash?

Othello   Is't lost? Is't gone? Speak: is it out o'the way?

Desdemona   Heaven bless us!

95 **Othello**   Say you?

Othello   That's bad. That handkerchief was given to my mother by an Egyptian. She was a clairvoyant, and could almost read people's thoughts. She told her that while she kept it, it would make her desirable, and ensure my father's lasting love. But if she lost it, or made a gift of it, my father would turn against her, and go looking for other women. On her deathbed she gave it to me, and told me to give it to my wife when that time came. I did so. Take heed: treat it as something very special, like your precious sight. To lose it, or to give it away, would be sinfulness without equal.

Desdemona   Is that possible?

Othello   It is true. There's magic woven into it. A sorceress two hundred years old sewed it in an inspired trance. The silkworms were sacred that bred the silk. It was dyed in a preparation made from mummy [*an essence usually made from embalmed bodies*] which experts distilled from maiden's hearts.

Desdemona   Indeed! Is this true?

Othello   Absolutely true. Therefore be extra careful.

Desdemona   Then would to God I'd never seen it!

Othello   Oh? Why?

Desdemona   Why do you speak so incoherently and wild?

Othello   Is it lost? Is it gone? Speak: have you got rid of it?

Desdemona   Heaven bless me!

Othello   What's your answer!

Desdemona   It is not lost.
But what an if it were?

Othello   How!

Desdemona   I say it is not lost.

100 **Othello**   Fetch't: let me see't.

Desdemona   Why, so I can, sir; but I will not now.
This is a trick to put me from my suit.
I pray let Cassio be received again.

Othello   Fetch me the handkerchief: my mind misgives.

105 **Desdemona**   Come, come:
You'll never meet a more sufficient man.

Othello   The handkerchief!

Desdemona   I pray, talk me of Cassio.

Othello   The handerkerchief!

110 **Desdemona**   A man that all his time
Hath founded his good fortunes on your love;
Shared dangers with you –

Othello   The handkerchief!

Desdemona   I'faith you are to blame.

115 **Othello**   Zounds!

                                              [*Exit*]

Emilia   Is not this man jealous?

Desdemona   I ne'er saw this before.
Sure, there's some wonder in this handkerchief:
I am most unhappy in the loss of it.

Desdemona   It isn't lost. But what if it were?

Othello   What?

Desdemona   I'm saying it's not lost.

Othello   Fetch it. Let me see it.

Desdemona   Well, so I can, sir, but I won't right now. This is a trick to side-step my request. Please see Cassio again.

Othello   Fetch me the handkerchief. I have misgivings.

Desdemona   Come, come. You'll never meet a more able man.

Othello   The handkerchief!

Desdemona   A man who has always depended on you, shared dangers with you –

Othello   The handkerchief!

Desdemona   Really, you're the one to blame!

Othello   In God's name!

   [*He storms out*]

Emilia   This man is jealous, surely?

Desdemona   I never saw him like this before. There must be something magical about this handkerchief. I'm most upset at losing it.

120 **Emilia**   'Tis not a year or two shows us a man.
They are all but stomachs, and we all but food;
They eat us hungerly, and when they are full,
They belch us. Look you, Cassio and my husband.

[*Enter* **Iago** *and* **Cassio**]

Iago   There is no other way: 'tis she must do it.
125   And lo, the happiness! Go, and importune her.

Desdemona   How now, good Cassio! What's the news
with you?

Cassio   Madam, my former suit. I do beseech you
That by your virtuous means I may again
130   Exist and be a member of his love,
Whom I, with all the office of my heart,
Entirely honour. I would not be delayed.
If my offence be of such mortal kind
That neither service past, nor present sorrows,
135   Nor purposed merit in futurity,
Can ransom me into his love again,
But to know so must be my benefit:
So shall I clothe me in a forced content,
And shut myself up in some other course
140   To fortune's alms.

Desdemona   Alas, thrice-gentle Cassio!
My advocation is not now in tune;
My lord is not my lord; nor should I know him,
Were he in favour as in humour altered.
145   So help me every spirit sanctified
As I have spoken for you all my best,
And stood within the blank of his displeasure
For my free speech! You must awhile be patient.
What I can do, I will; and more I will,
150   Than for myself I dare. Let that suffice you.

180

Emilia   It doesn't take long for a man to reveal
himself. They are walking stomachs, and we are
nothing but their food. They gobble us up, and
when they're full, they belch us out. Look – Cassio
and my husband.

[**Iago** *enters with* **Cassio**]

Iago   There is no other way. She must do it for you.
And then – good luck! Go and plead with her.

Desdemona   Greetings, good Cassio! What now?

Cassio   Madam, it's my old request. I'm asking that
by means of your good offices I may again be
recognized and loved again by one whom I honour
from the bottom of my heart. I can wait no longer. If
my offence is so fatal that neither my past service,
my present remorse, nor my future good intentions
can redeem me in his favour, it can only be to my
benefit to know. Then I'll resign myself to it, and try
my luck elsewhere.

Desdemona   Alas, most noble Cassio, this wouldn't
be the right time. My husband is not himself. I
wouldn't recognize him if his looks were as changed
as his mood. Heaven knows I have spoken for you
as best I could, and been the target of his
displeasure for speaking so freely! You must be
patient a while longer. What I can do, I will: I'll do
more than I dare do for myself. Let that suffice you.

Iago   Is my lord angry?

Emilia   He went hence but now
And certainly in strange unquietness.

Iago   Can he be angry? I have seen the cannon
155   When it hath blown his ranks into the air,
And like the devil from his very arm
Puffed his own brother: and can he be angry?
Something of moment then. I will go meet him.
There's matter in't indeed if he be angry.

160 **Desdemona**   I prithee do so.

                                          [*Exit* **Iago**]

                           Something sure of state,
Either from Venice, or some unhatched practice
Made demonstrable here in Cyprus to him,
Hath puddled his clear spirit; and in such cases
165   Men's natures wrangle with inferior things,
Though great ones are their object. 'Tis even so.
For let our finger ache, and it endues
Our healthful members even to that sense
Of pain. Nay, we must think men are not gods,
170   Nor of them look for such observances
As fits the bridal. Beshrew me much, Emilia,
I was – unhandsome warrior as I am –
Arraigning his unkindness with my soul;
But now I find I had suborned the witness
175   And he's indicted falsely.

Emilia   Pray heaven it be state matters, as you think,
And no conception nor no jealous toy
Concerning you.

Desdemona   Alas the day! I never gave him cause!

Iago Is my lord angry?

Emilia He's just gone, and certainly he's strangely disturbed.

Iago Can he be angry? I've seen cannon blow his soldiers into the air, and like the devil, carry off his own brother from his side – and can he be angry? It must be something very important. I'll go to him. It is indeed serious if he's angry.

Desdemona Please do.

[**Iago** *goes*]

Surely some political matter – either to do with Venice, or a secret plot revealed to him here in Cyprus – has clouded his mind. In such circumstances, men tend to wrangle over minor things, though major ones are really their target. That's what it is. An aching finger makes the rest of our bodies sensitive to pain. No, we must remember that men are not gods, and mustn't expect the same tenderness as befits the wedding. Shame on me, Emilia! Poor soldier that I am, I was allowing my feelings to charge him with unkindness. Now I realize I am a prejudiced witness, and he is falsely accused.

Emilia Pray heaven it is politics, as you think, and no fantasy or jealous notion concerning you.

Desdemona Oh grief! I never gave him any pretext!

180 **Emilia**   But jealous souls will not be answered so;
     They are not ever jealous for the cause,
     But jealous for they are jealous. It is a monster
     Begot upon itself, born on itself.

   Desdemona   Heaven keep that monster from Othello's
185   mind!

   Emilia   Lady, amen.

   Desdemona   I will go seek him. Cassio, walk here about.
     If I do find him fit, I'll move your suit,
     And seek to effect it to my uttermost.

190 **Cassio**   I humbly thank your ladyship.

                         [*Exeunt* **Desdemona** *and* **Emilia**]

     [*Enter* **Bianca**]

   Bianca   Save you, friend Cassio.

   Cassio   What make you from home?
     How is it with you, my most fair Bianca?
     I'faith, sweet love, I was coming to your house.

195 **Bianca**   And I was going to your lodging, Cassio.
     What, keep a week away? Seven days and nights?
     Eight score eight hours? And lovers' absent hours
     More tedious than the dial eight score times!
     Oh weary reckoning!

200 **Cassio**   Pardon me, Bianca.
     I have this while with leaden thoughts been pressed:
     But I shall in a more convenient time
     Strike off this score of absence. Sweet Bianca,
     Take me this work out.

Emilia   Jealous folk won't take that for an answer.
They are never jealous on account of fact. They are
jealous because they are jealous. It is a monster,
self-conceived, born of itself.

Desdemona   Heaven keep that monster from Othello's
mind!

Emilia   Madam, amen to that!

Desdemona   I'll go and find him. Cassio, stay round
here. If he's in the right mood, I'll put your case to
him, and do my utmost to succeed.

Cassio   My grateful thanks.

[**Desdemona** *and* **Emilia** *leave*]

[**Bianca**, *the mistress of* **Michael Cassio**, *enters*]

Bianca   Greetings, friend Cassio!

Cassio   What are you doing out and about? How are
you, my most beautiful Bianca? Actually,
sweetheart, I was coming to your house.

Bianca   And I was going to your lodging, Cassio.
What! Keep away a week? Seven days and nights?
Eight score plus eight hours? Hours when lovers are
parted are eight score times more tedious than real
time . . . Oh, such a wearisome calculation!

Cassio   Forgive me, Bianca. I've been very depressed
all this while. At a more appropriate time I'll make
this absence good. Sweet Bianca, copy this for me.
[*He hands her* **Desdemona's** *handkerchief*]

205 **Bianca**   Oh Cassio, whence came this?
    This is some token from a newer friend.
    To the felt absence now I feel a cause.
    Is't come to this?

    Cassio   Go to, woman!
210 Throw your vile guesses in the devil's teeth
     From whence you have them. You are jealous now
     That this is from some mistress, some remembrance:
     No, by my faith, Bianca.

    Bianca   Why, whose is it?

215 **Cassio**   I know not, sweet. I found it in my chamber.
     I like the work well. Ere it be demanded –
     As like enough it will – I'd have it copied.
     Take it and do't, and leave me for this time.

    Bianca   Leave you? Wherefore?

220 **Cassio**   I do attend here on the General,
     And think it no addition, nor my wish,
     To have him see me womaned.

    Bianca   Why, I pray you?

    Cassio   Not that I love you not.

225 **Bianca**   But that you do not love me.
     I pray you, bring me on the way a little,
     And say if I shall see you soon at night.

    Cassio   'Tis but a little way that I can bring you,
     For I attend here: but I'll see you soon.

230 **Bianca**   'Tis very good. I must be circumstanced.

                                        [*Exeunt*]

Bianca   Oh Cassio, where did you get this? This is a love-token from a new girl-friend. To the hurtful absence I now can add a reason. Is this how things are?

Cassio   Don't be silly, woman! Throw your vile suspicions back in the devil's teeth, where you got them. You're jealous now because you think this is from some sweetheart; a love-token. No, honestly, Bianca!

Bianca   Well then, whose is it?

Cassio   I don't know, sweetie. I found it in my room. The design pleases me. Before it is claimed – as sure enough it will be – I'd like to have it copied. Take it and do it, and leave me for now.

Bianca   Leave you? Why?

Cassio   I'm waiting for the General, and I don't think it would be helpful, nor would it be my wish, to have him see me with a woman.

Bianca   Why, may I ask?

Cassio   Not that I do not love you.

Bianca   Just that you love me not! Walk with me a little, and tell me if I'll see you one night, soon.

Cassio   I can't go far, as I have to wait here. But I'll see you soon.

Bianca   All right. I'll have to be content with that.

[*They go*]

Act four

Scene 1

Cyprus. Before the Castle. Enter **Othello** *and* **Iago**.

Iago Will you think so?

Othello   Think so, Iago?

Iago   What;
  To kiss in private?

5 **Othello**   An unauthorised kiss.

Iago Or to be naked with her friend in bed
  An hour or more, not meaning any harm?

Othello Naked in bed, Iago, and not mean harm?
  It is hypocrisy against the devil.
10   They that mean virtuously and yet do so,
  The devil their virtue tempts, and they tempt heaven.

Iago So they do nothing, 'tis a venial slip;
  But if I give my wife a handkerchief –

Othello What then?

15 **Iago** Why then 'tis hers, my lord, and being hers,
  She may, I think, bestow't on any man.

Othello She is protectress of her honour too.
  May she give that?

Iago Her honour is an essence that's not seen;
20   They have it very oft that have it not.
  But, for the handkerchief –

Act four

Scene 1

Enter **Othello** *and* **Iago**.

Iago   Do you think so?

Othello   Think so, Iago?

Iago   What, to kiss in private?

Othello   An unauthorised kiss!

Iago   Or to be naked with her 'friend' in bed, an hour or more, not meaning any harm?

Othello   Naked in bed, Iago, and not mean harm? That is hypocrisy versus the devil. Those with virtuous intentions who do that – the devil tempts their virtue, and they tempt heaven not to interfere.

Iago   If they do nothing, it's a pardonable error. But if I give my wife a handkerchief –

Othello   What then?

Iago   Why then, it's hers, my lord, and being hers, she may, I think, give it to any man.

Othello   She is in charge of her honour too. Can she give that away?

Iago   Her honour is a quality you can't see. People often seem to have it when they haven't. As for the handkerchief . . .

Othello   By heaven, I would most gladly have forgot it!
Thou said'st – oh, it comes o'er my memory
As doth the raven o'er the infected house,
25   Boding to all – he had my handkerchief.

Iago   Ay, what of that?

Othello   That's not so good now.

Iago   What
If I had said I had seen him do you wrong,
30   Or heard him say – as knaves be such abroad,
Who having by their own importunate suit
Or voluntary dotage of some mistress
Convinced or supplied them, cannot choose
But they must blab –

35 **Othello**   Hath he said anything?

Iago   He hath, my lord; but be you well assured,
No more than he'll unswear.

Othello   What hath he said?

Iago   Faith, that he did – I know not what he did.

40 **Othello**   But what?

Iago   Lie.

Othello   With her?

Iago   With her, on her, what you will.

Othello   Lie with her? Lie on her? We say lie on her when
45   they belie her. Lie with her! Zounds, that's fulsome!
Handkerchief – confessions – handkerchief! To confess
and be hanged for his labour. First, to be hanged and
then to confess! I tremble at it. Nature would not invest
herself in such shadowing passion without some
50   instruction. It is not words that shake me thus! Pish!

Othello   By heaven, I'd gladly have forgotten it! You said – oh, it returns to my memory like the raven that flies over plague-stricken houses, threatening everyone – that he had my handkerchief!

Iago   Yes. But what of that?

Othello   That doesn't sound so good now.

Iago   Supposing I had said I'd seen him on the job? Or heard him say – since womanizers can't resist boasting in public after they've scored, either through seduction or because an infatuated girl-friend has obliged them –

Othello   Has he said anything?

Iago   He has, my lord. But you can be quite certain he'd deny it all.

Othello   What has he said?

Iago   'Strewth, that he – I don't know what he did.

Othello   What?

Iago   Lie . . .

Othello   With her?

Iago   With her – on her – what you will.

Othello   Lie with her? Lie on her? They say 'lie on her' when they mean 'she's layed'. Lie with her . . .! God, that's disgusting! Handkerchief . . . confession . . . handkerchief . . .! Confess, and be hanged! No, hanged first, confess later! I tremble at the thought: nature doesn't cloud the mind without good reason. Words alone would not rattle me like this!

Noses, ears, and lips! Is't possible? – Confess?
Handkerchief! Oh devil!

[*He falls in a trance*]

Iago   Work on,
My medicine, work! Thus credulous fools are caught,
55   And many worthy and chaste dames even thus,
All guiltless, meet reproach. What ho, my lord!
My lord, I say! Othello!

[*Enter* **Cassio**]

How now, Cassio!

Cassio   What's the matter?

Iago   My lord is fallen into an epilepsy.
60   This is his second fit. He had one yesterday.

Cassio   Rub him about the temples.

Iago   No, forbear.
The lethargy must have his quiet course.
If not, he foams at mouth; and by and by
65   Breaks out to savage madness. Look, he stirs.
Do you withdraw yourself a little while:
He will recover straight. When he is gone,
I would on great occasion speak with you.

[*Exit* **Cassio**]

How is it, General? Have you not hurt your head?

70   **Othello**   Dost thou mock me?

Iago   I mock you? No, by heaven!
Would you would bear your fortune like a man!

Othello   A horned man's a monster and a beast.

[*Thoughts of adultery nauseate him*] Pah! Noses –
ears – and lips! Is it possible! Confess?
Handkerchief? Oh, devil!

[*He collapses in a fit*]

Iago   Keep working, my medicine, keep on working!
This is how credulous fools are duped, and how
many decent and chaste women – all innocent –
lose their reputations! [*Shaking* **Othello**] My lord!
My lord! Othello!

[**Cassio** *enters*]

Greetings, Cassio!

Cassio   What's the matter?

Iago   My lord has had an epileptic fit. It's his second.
He had one yesterday.

Cassio   Rub his temples.

Iago   No, don't! The fit must run its course quietly. If
not, he foams at the mouth, and by and by breaks
out into uncontrolled madness. Look, he's coming
round. Leave us for a while. He'll be all right soon.
When he has gone, I'd like to speak to you about
something important.

[**Cassio** *goes*]

How are you, General? Have you hurt your head?

Othello   Are you mocking me?

Iago   Mocking you? No, by heaven! I wish you would
take your troubles like a man!

Othello   A man with a loose wife is a monster and a
beast! [*because he was said to 'wear horns'*]

Iago   There's many a beast then in a populous city,
75   And many a civil monster.

Othello   Did he confess?

Iago   Good sir, be a man.
   Think every bearded fellow that's but yoked
   May draw with you. There's millions now alive
80   That nightly lie in those unproper beds
   Which they dare swear peculiar. Your case is better.
   Oh, 'tis the spite of hell, the fiend's arch-mock,
   To lip a wanton in a secure couch,
   And to suppose her chaste! No, let me know;
85   And knowing what I am, I know what she shall be.

Othello   Oh, thou art wise, 'tis certain.

Iago   Stand you awhile apart;
   Confine yourself but in a patient list.
   Whilst you were here erewhile, mad with your grief –
90   A passion most unsuiting such a man –
   Cassio came hither. I shifted him away
   And laid good 'scuse upon your ecstasy;
   Bade him anon return and here speak with me,
   The which he promised. Do but encave yourself,
95   And mark the jeers, the gibes, and notable scorns
   That dwell in every region of his face.
   For I will make him tell the tale anew,
   Where, how, how oft, how long ago, and when
   He has, and is again, to cope your wife.
100   I say, but mark his gestures. Marry, patience!
   Or I shall say you're all in all in spleen
   And nothing of a man.

Othello   Dost thou hear, Iago?
   I will be found most cunning in my patience,
105   But – dost thou hear? – most bloody.

Iago   Then there's many a beast in a populous city, and many a citizen monster!

Othello   Did he confess?

Iago   Good sir, be a man. Every married man is in your position. There are millions now living who sleep each night in adulterous beds, believing they have sole rights. Your situation is better. Oh, it's the vengeance of hell, the fiend's best joke, to make love to a harlot in a care-free bed, thinking she's chaste! No. I'd rather know. And knowing what I'm like, I know what would happen to her!

Othello   Oh, you're a wise fellow, that's for sure.

Iago   Step aside for a moment. Pull yourself together. While you were here just now, mad with grief – a passion unsuited to such a man as you – Cassio came. I got rid of him and made a plausible excuse for your malady. I told him to return soon and speak to me here, which he promised to do. Conceal yourself, and note the sneers, the gibes, the obvious signs of scorn in every corner of his face. I'll make him go through the story afresh – where; how; how often; how recently; and when he has tupped your wife and is due to do so again. Just note his reactions I tell you! And keep yourself under control, now – or I'll say you are crazy with anger and no man.

Othello   Do you hear, Iago? I'll be deviously cunning in my patience but – do you hear? – ruthlessly bloody.

Iago   That's not amiss,
But yet keep time in all. Will you withdraw?

                                    [**Othello** *withdraws*]

Now will I question Cassio of Bianca;
A housewife, that by selling her desires
110   Buys herself bread and clothes. It is a creature
That dotes on Cassio, as 'tis the strumpet's plague
To beguile many and be beguiled by one.
He, when he hears of her, cannot refrain
From the excess of laughter. Here he comes.
115   As he shall smile, Othello shall go mad;
And his unbookish jealousy must construe
Poor Cassio's smiles, gestures, and light behaviour
Quite in the wrong.

     [*Enter* **Cassio**]

                              How do you now, Lieutenant?

120 **Cassio**   The worser that you give me the addition,
Whose want even kills me.

   Iago   Ply Desdemona well and you are sure on't.
Now if this suit lay in Bianca's power,
How quickly should you speed!

125 **Cassio**   Alas, poor caitiff!

   Othello   Look how he laughs already!

   Iago   I never knew a woman love man so.

   Cassio   Alas, poor rogue; I think i'faith she loves me.

   Othello   Now he denies it faintly, and laughs it out.

130 **Iago**   Do you hear, Cassio?

Iago   That's in order, but keep control of yourself. Will you withdraw?

[**Othello** *conceals himself*]

Now I'll question Cassio about Bianca, a hussy who earns her living selling her body. She's a creature who dotes on Cassio – it's the strumpet's occupational hazard to delude the many and to be duped herself by one. When he hears talk of her, he can't stop roaring with laughter. Here he comes.

[**Cassio** *enters*]

As he smiles, Othello will go mad. In his jealous ignorance, he will construe poor Cassio's smiles, gestures and light-hearted behaviour quite wrongly. How are you now, Lieutenant?

Cassio   All the worse for giving me a title the loss of which is killing me.

Iago   Keep on at Desdemona and you are sure to get it back. Now if Bianca had any say in the matter, how quickly you would prosper!

Cassio   [*smiling*] Alas, poor wretch!

Othello   [*aside*] Look how he's laughing already!

Iago   I never knew a woman love a man so much.

Cassio   [*amused*] Alas, the little villain. I believe she does love me indeed.

Othello   [*aside*] Now he pretends to deny it, and laughs it off.

Iago   Do you know, Cassio –

Othello   Now he importunes him to tell it on.
Go to, well said, well said!

Iago   She gives it out that you shall marry her.
Do you intend it?

135 **Cassio**   Ha, ha, ha!

Othello   Do you triumph, Roman? Do you triumph?

Cassio   I marry her! What, a customer? Prithee bear some
charity to my wits. Do not think it so unwholesome. Ha,
ha, ha!

140 **Othello**   So, so, so, so: they laugh that win.

Iago   Faith, the cry goes that you shall marry her.

Cassio   Prithee, say true.

Iago   I am a very villain else.

Othello   Have you scored me? Well.

145 **Cassio**   This is the monkey's own giving out. She is
persuaded I will marry her out of her own love and
flattery, not out of my promise.

Othello   Iago beckons me. Now he begins the story.

Cassio   She was here even now. She haunts me in every
150   place. I was the other day talking on the sea-bank with
certain Venetians, and thither comes the bauble. By this
hand, she falls thus about my neck –

Othello   Crying 'Oh dear Cassio!' as it were. His gesture
imports it.

Othello   [*aside*] Now he's getting him to tell his story. Go on! Well said, well said!

Iago   She tells everybody that you're going to marry her. Do you intend to?

Cassio   [*a huge joke*] Ha, ha, ha!

Othello   [*aside*] Are you crowing, Mr Cock-sure? Are you crowing?

Cassio   I marry her! What? A harlot? Give me credit for some sense. Don't think I'm that stupid! Ha, ha, ha!

Othello   [*aside*] So, so, so, so. He who laughs last . . .

Iago   'Strewth, rumour has it that you'll marry her.

Cassio   Oh, come on!

Iago   Call me a villain else!

Othello   [*aside*] Have you bested me? Well . . .

Cassio   This is what the little monkey's saying. She's convinced I'll marry her because she's so in love with me, not because I've said I will.

Othello   [*aside*] Iago beckons to me. Now he's getting to the point.

Cassio   She was here just now. She haunts me everywhere. I was talking on the seashore with some Venetians the other day, and the silly girl comes and – I tell you no lie – she throws her arms round my neck!

Othello   [*aside*] Crying 'Oh darling Cassio' as it were. His gesture implies it.

155 **Cassio**   So hangs and lolls and weeps upon me, so shakes
   and pulls me. Ha, ha, ha!

Othello   Now he tells how she plucked him to my
   chamber. I see that nose of yours, but not that dog I
   shall throw it to!

160 **Cassio**   Well, I must leave her company.

Iago   Before me! Look where she comes.

Cassio   'Tis such another fitchew! Marry, a perfumed one!

[*Enter* **Bianca**]

What do you mean by this haunting of me?

Bianca   Let the devil and his dam haunt you! What did
165   you mean by that same handkerchief you gave me even
   now? I was a fine fool to take it. I must take out the
   work! A likely piece of work, that you should find it in
   your chamber, and not know who left it there! This is
   some minx's token, and I must take out the work?
170   There, give it your hobby-horse, wheresoever you had it.
   I'll take out no work on't.

Cassio   How now, my sweet Bianca! How now, how now!

Othello   By heaven, that should be my handkerchief!

Bianca   If you'll come to supper tonight, you may. If you
175   will not, come when you are next prepared for.

[*Exit*]

Iago   After her, after her!

Cassio   Faith I must: she'll rail in the street else.

Iago   Will you sup there?

Cassio She hangs and lolls and weeps over me, hauls and pulls me about. Ha, ha, ha!

Othello [*aside*] Now he's describing how she dragged him to my bedroom. Oh, I can see that nose of yours, if not the dog I'll throw it to!

Cassio Well, I'll have to break with her.

Iago Fancy that! Look, here she comes!

Cassio A pole-cat, no less! [*They were renowned for lechery*] A perfumed one!

[**Bianca** *enters*]

What do you mean by haunting me like this?

Bianca Let the devil and his wife haunt you! What did *you* mean by that handkerchief you gave me just now? I was a fine fool to take it. 'I must copy it!' A likely story, that you found it in your room, and didn't know who left it there! This is some scrubber's love-token, and I must copy it? There [*she hands it back*], give it to your fancy-woman, wherever you got it. I'm not copying it.

Cassio Now, now, my sweet Bianca! Now, now!

Othello [*aside*] By heaven, that's my handkerchief!

Bianca If you want to come to dinner tonight, you can. If you don't, come when you're next invited.

[*She flounces out*]

Iago Go after her, after her!

Cassio Indeed I must. She'll have the street up, otherwise.

Iago Will you dine there?

Cassio   Faith, I intend to.

180 **Iago**   Well, I may chance to see you, for I would very fain speak with you.

Cassio   Prithee come, will you?

Iago   Go to! Say no more.

[*Exit* **Cassio**]

Othello   [*coming forward*] How shall I murder him, Iago?

185 **Iago**   Did you perceive how he laughed at his vice?

Othello   Oh, Iago!

Iago   And did you see the handkerchief?

Othello   Was that mine?

Iago   Yours, by this hand! And to see how he prizes the
190   foolish woman your wife: she gave it him, and he hath given it his whore.

Othello   I would have him nine years a-killing! A fine woman, a fair woman, a sweet woman!

Iago   Nay, you must forget that.

195 **Othello**   Ay, let her rot and perish, and be damned tonight, for she shall not live! No, my heart is turned to stone: I strike it, and it hurts my hand. Oh, the world has not a sweeter creature! She might lie by an emperor's side and command him tasks.

200 **Iago**   Nay, that's not your way.

Cassio   Indeed, I intend to.

Iago   Well, I may see you. I'd really like to talk to you.

Cassio   Join me, will you?

Iago   Perhaps. Say no more.

[**Cassio** *leaves*]

Othello   [*Coming out of hiding*] How shall I murder him, Iago?

Iago   Did you notice how he laughed at his wickedness?

Othello   Oh, Iago!

Iago   And did you see the handkerchief?

Othello   Was that mine?

Iago   Yours, without a doubt. And see how much he values the foolish woman, your wife. She gave it to him, and he has given it to his whore.

Othello   I'd have him linger for nine years in his dying! A fine woman . . . a beautiful woman . . . a sweet woman . . .!

Iago   Now, you must forget that.

Othello   Yes: let her rot and perish, and be damned tonight; because she must not live! No. My heart is turned to stone. [*He beats his breast*] I strike it, and it hurts my hand. Oh, the world has not a sweeter creature! She could be at the side of an Emperor, and have him running errands.

Iago   But that's not your way . . .

Othello   Hang her! I do but say what she is: so delicate with her needle, an admirable musician! Oh, she will sing the savageness out of a bear! Of so high and plenteous wit and invention!

205 **Iago**   She's the worse for all this.

Othello   A thousand, thousand times! And then of so gentle a condition.

Iago   Ay, too gentle.

Othello   Nay, that's certain: but yet the pity of it, Iago!
210   Oh, Iago, the pity of it, Iago!

Iago   If you are so fond over her iniquity, give her patent to offend, for if it touches not you, it comes near nobody.

Othello   I will chop her into messes! Cuckold me!

Iago   Oh, 'tis foul in her!

215 **Othello**   With mine officer!

Iago   That's fouler.

Othello   Get me some poison, Iago, this night. I'll not expostulate with her, lest her body and beauty unprovide my mind again. This night, Iago.

220 **Iago**   Do it not with poison. Strangle her in her bed, even the bed she hath contaminated.

Othello   Good, good! The justice of it pleases; very good!

Iago   And for Cassio, let me be his undertaker. You shall hear more by midnight.

Othello   Hang her! I'm only saying what she is; so skilled with a needle, and an admirable musician! Oh, she could tame a savage bear with her singing! She has such high and plentiful intelligence, and imagination!

Iago   She's the worse for it all.

Othello   Oh, a thousand, thousand times! And then so well-bred!

Iago   Yes, too well-bred.

Othello   Oh yes, that's true. But still, the pity of it, Iago! Oh Iago, the pity of it, Iago!

Iago   If you're so fond of her misbehaviour, why not give her a licence to offend? If you're not bothered, nobody else will be.

Othello   I'll chop her into little pieces! To be unfaithful to me!

Iago   Oh, it's foul of her!

Othello   With my Lieutenant!

Iago   Even fouler.

Othello   Get me some poison, Iago, tonight. I won't argue with her, in case her body and her beauty weaken my resolution. Tonight, Iago!

Iago   Don't do it with poison. Strangle her in her bed – the very bed she has contaminated.

Othello   Good, good! I like the irony of it. Very good!

Iago   As for Cassio, I'll look after him. You'll hear more by midnight.

225 **Othello**   Excellent good!

[*A trumpet sounds within*]

What trumpet is that same?

[*Enter* **Lodovico, Desdemona,** *and Attendants*]

Iago   'Tis Lodovico,
Come from the Duke; and see, your wife is with him.

Lodovico   God save you, worthy General!

230 **Othello**   With all my heart, sir.

Lodovico   The Duke and Senators of Venice greet you.

[*He gives him a letter*]

Othello   I kiss the instrument of their pleasure.

[*He opens the letter, and reads*]

Desdemona   And what's the news, good cousin Lodovico?

Iago   I am very glad to see you, signor:
235   Welcome to Cyprus.

Lodovico   I thank you. How does Lieutenant Cassio?

Iago   Lives, sir.

Desdemona   Cousin, there's fallen between him and my
      lord
240   An unkind breach; but you shall make all well.

Othello   Are you sure of that?

Desdemona   My lord?

Othello   'This fail you not to do, as you will' –

Othello   Splendid!

[*A trumpet sounds*]

What's that trumpet?

Iago   Something from Venice, I'll be bound.

[**Lodovico**, *a member of* **Brabantio's** *family, enters with* **Desdemona** *and Attendants*]

Lodovico   God save you, worthy general!

Othello   With all my heart, sir.

Lodovico   The Duke and Senators of Venice greet you.

[*He gives* **Othello** *a letter*]

Othello   [*putting it to his lips as a sign of loyalty*] I kiss their commands. [*He opens it and reads the contents*]

Desdemona   And what's the news, cousin Lodovico?

Iago   I am very glad to see you, Signor. Welcome to Cyprus.

Lodovico   Thank you. How's Lieutenant Cassio?

Iago   He lives, sir.

Desdemona   Cousin, there's been some unfortunate trouble between him and my lord. But you can put things right.

Othello   [*aside*] Are you so sure?

Desdemona   My lord?

Othello   [*reverting quickly to the letter*] 'Do not fail to do this, or else you will –'

Lodovico   He did not call; he's busy in the paper.
245   Is there division 'twixt my lord and Cassio?

Desdemona   A most unhappy one; I would do much
To atone them, for the love I bear to Cassio.

Othello   Fire and brimstone!

Desdemona   My lord?

250 **Othello**   Are you wise?

Desdemona   What, is he angry?

Lodovico   Maybe the letter moved him.
For, as I think, they do command him home,
Deputing Cassio in his government.

255 **Desdemona**   By my troth, I am glad on't.

Othello   Indeed!

Desdemona   My lord?

Othello   I am glad to see you mad.

Desdemona   Why, sweet Othello!

260 **Othello**   Devil!

[*He strikes her*]

Desdemona   I have not deserved this.

Lodovico   My lord, this would not be believed in Venice,
Though I should swear I saw't. 'Tis very much.
Make her amends; she weeps.

265 **Othello**   Oh devil, devil!
If that the earth could teem with woman's tears,
Each drop she falls would prove a crocodile.
Out of my sight!

Lodovico   He didn't call to you. He's engrossed in the document. Is there a split between my lord and Cassio?

Desdemona   A most unhappy one. I'd do a lot to reconcile them because I like Cassio.

Othello   [*aside*] Hell and damnation!

Desdemona   My lord?

Othello   [*aside*] Are you in your right mind?

Desdemona   What, is he angry?

Lodovico   Perhaps the letter upset him. I rather think they have ordered him home, appointing Cassio to stand in for him.

Desdemona   Believe me, I'm glad.

Othello   [*aside*] Indeed!

Desdemona   [*going to him*] My lord?

Othello   I'm glad you exposed your madness!

Desdemona   [*shocked*] Why, sweet Othello!

Othello   Devil!

[*He slaps her across the face*]

Desdemona   I have not deserved this!

Lodovico   My lord, this would not be believed in Venice, if I swore I'd seen it with my own eyes! It's too much. Make up with her. She's crying.

Othello   Oh, devil, devil! If women's tears could make the earth conceive, she would give birth to crocodiles! Get out of my sight!

Desdemona   I will not stay to offend you.

270 **Lodovico**   Truly, an obedient lady.
I do beseech your lordship, call her back.

Othello   Mistress!

Desdemona   My lord?

Othello   What would you with her, sir?

275 **Lodovico**   Who? I, my lord?

Othello   Ay, you did wish that I would make her turn.
Sir, she can turn, and turn, and yet go on,
And turn again. And she can weep, sir, weep.
And she's obedient; as you say, obedient;
280   Very obedient. Proceed you in your tears.
Concerning this, sir – oh, well-painted passion! –
I am commanded home – Get you away!
I'll send for you anon. – Sir, I obey the mandate,
And will return to Venice. – Hence, avaunt!

                              [*Exit* **Desdemona**]

285   Cassio shall have my place. And sir, tonight
I do entreat that we may sup together.
You are welcome, sir, to Cyprus. Goats and monkeys!

                              [*Exit*]

Lodovico   Is this the noble Moor, whom our full senate
Call all-in-all sufficient? Is this the nature
290   Whom passion could not shake? Whose solid virtue
The shot of accident nor dart of chance
Could neither graze nor pierce?

Desdemona   I won't stay to offend you . . . [*She turns to go*]

Lodovico   Truly an obedient lady. I beg your lordship to call her back.

Othello   Madam!

Desdemona   [*turning*] My lord?

Othello   What do you want with her, sir?

Lodovico   Who, I, my lord?

Othello   Yes. You wanted me to make her turn around. Sir, she can turn, and turn, and still go on and turn again. And she can weep, sir, weep. And she's obedient. As you said yourself, obedient. Very obedient. [*To* **Desdemona**] Carry on crying. [*To* **Lodovico**, *flicking the letter*] Concerning this, sir – [*To* **Desdemona**] Oh, what convincing grief! [*To* **Lodovico**] I am ordered home – [*To* **Desdemona**] Go away! I'll send for you afterwards – [*To* **Lodovico**] Sir, I obey orders and will return to Venice. [*To* **Desdemona**] Get out! Go!

[**Desdemona** *leaves, distressed*]

Cassio can take over my command. And, sir, I hope that we can dine together tonight. You are welcome, sir, to Cyprus. [*His personal obsession takes over again*] Goats and monkeys!

[*He goes*]

Lodovico   Is this the noble Moor who has our entire Senate's total confidence? Is this the nature that has never known anger? Whose solid reliability could never be affected by the unforeseen, or the unlucky?

Iago   He is much changed.

Lodovico   Are his wits safe? Is he not light of brain?

295 **Iago**   He's that he is: I may not breathe my censure
What he might be. If as he might, he is not,
I would to heaven he were.

Lodovico   What! Strike his wife?

Iago   Faith, that was not so well: yet would I knew
300   That stroke would prove the worst!

Lodovico   Is it his use?
Or did the letters work upon his blood
And new-create this fault?

Iago   Alas, alas!
305   It is not honesty in me to speak
What I have seen and known. You shall observe him,
And his own courses will denote him so,
That I may save my speech. Do but go after,
And mark how he continues.

310 **Lodovico**   I am sorry that I am deceived in him.

                                        [*Exeunt*]

Scene 2

Cyprus. The Castle. Enter **Othello** *and* **Emilia**.

Othello   You have seen nothing?

Emilia   Nor ever heard, nor ever did suspect.

Othello   Yes, and you have seen Cassio and she together.

Iago   He is much changed.

Lodovico   Has he lost his wits? Is he out of his mind?

Iago   He is what he is. I cannot go so far as to say
what's wrong. If he is not what he should be, I
would to heaven he were.

Lodovico   But strike his wife!

Iago   Indeed, that wasn't good enough. Yet I wish I
could be sure that blow would prove to be his
worst!

Lodovico   Is this typical, or did the letter anger him
and set him off afresh?

Iago   Alas, alas! It's disloyal of me to say what I have
seen and what I know. You must observe him, and
his behaviour will tell you everything; that way I
need say nothing. Follow him and notice how he
behaves.

Lodovico   I'm sorry that I've been so deceived in him.

[*They go*]

Scene 2

Othello *enters with* **Emilia**. *Throughout the scene he
treats her like a maid in a brothel.*

Othello   You have seen nothing, then?

Emilia   No. Nor heard, or ever suspected.

Othello   Yes: you've seen Cassio and her together!

Emilia But then I saw no harm; and then I heard
5   Each syllable that breath made up between them.

Othello What; did they never whisper?

Emilia   Never, my lord.

Othello Nor send you out o'the way?

Emilia   Never.

10 **Othello** To fetch her fan, her gloves, her mask, nor
nothing?

Emilia Never, my lord.

Othello That's strange.

Emilia I durst, my lord, to wager she is honest,
15   Lay down my soul at stake: if you think other,
Remove your thought; it doth abuse your bosom.
If any wretch have put this in your head,
Let heaven requite it with the serpent's curse!
For if she be not honest, chaste, and true,
20   There's no man happy. The purest of her sex
Is foul as slander.

Othello   Bid her come hither. Go!

[*Exit* **Emilia**]

She says enough; yet she's a simple bawd
That cannot say as much. This is a subtle whore,
25   A closet, lock and key, of villainous secrets;
And yet she'll kneel and pray. I have seen her do't.

[*Enter* **Desdemona** *and* **Emilia**]

Desdemona My lord, what is your will?

Othello   Pray, chuck, come hither.

Desdemona What is your pleasure?

Emilia   But I saw no harm. And I heard every syllable they uttered.

Othello   What! Did they never whisper?

Emilia   Never, my lord.

Othello   Or send you out of the way?

Emilia   Never.

Othello   To fetch her fan, her gloves, her veil, or anything?

Emilia   Never, my lord.

Othello   That's strange . . .

Emilia   My lord, I'd wager my soul that she is faithful. If you think otherwise, forget it: it's coming between you and your peace. If some wretch has put the idea in your head, may God put a curse on him like he did on the serpent! If she's not faithful, chaste and true, no man can be happy. The purest of women would be as foul as slander is.

Othello   Tell her to come here. Go!

[**Emilia** *leaves*]

She says the right things, but she'd be a poor bawd that couldn't say the same. My wife's a subtle whore: a locked store-room of villainous secrets. Nonetheless, she'll kneel and pray. I've seen her do it.

[**Desdemona** *and* **Emilia** *enter*]

Desdemona   My lord, what is your wish?

Othello   Chick – come here, will you?

Desdemona   What can I do for you?

215

30 **Othello**   Let me see your eyes.
       Look in my face.

Desdemona   What horrible fancy's this?

Othello   [*to* **Emilia**] Some of your function, mistress.
       Leave procreants alone and shut the door.
35   Cough or cry 'hem' if anybody come.
       Your mystery, your mystery! Nay, dispatch!

                                              [*Exit* **Emilia**]

Desdemona   Upon my knees, what doth your speech
       import?
       I understand a fury in your words,
40   But not the words.

Othello   Why, what art thou?

Desdemona   Your wife, my lord. Your true and loyal
       wife.

Othello   Come, swear it. Damn thyself,
45   Lest being like one of heaven, the devils themselves
       Should fear to seize thee. Therefore be double-damned:
       Swear thou art honest.

Desdemona   Heaven doth truly know it.

Othello   Heaven truly knows that thou art false as hell!

50 **Desdemona**   To whom, my lord? With whom? How am I
       false?

 ⌜**Othello**   Ah, Desdemona! Away, away, away!

Desdemona   Alas, the heavy day! Why do you weep?
       Am I the motive of these tears, my lord?
55   If haply you my father do suspect
       As instrument of this your calling back.
       Lay not your blame on me. If you have lost him,
       I have lost him too.

216

Othello   Let me see your eyes. Look in my face.

Desdemona   Whatever is the matter?

Othello   [*to* **Emilia**] Be about your business, miss.
Leave mating couples alone and shut the door.
Cough, or cry 'ahem!' if anyone comes. To your
calling! Your trade! Jump to it!

[**Emilia** *goes*]

Desdemona   Upon my knees, what are you trying to
say? I understand the anger of your words, but not
their meaning.

Othello   Why, what are you?

Desdemona   Your wife, my lord! Your true and loyal
wife.

Othello   Come. Swear it! Damn yourself – in case
your angelic looks make the devils too scared to
seize you! Therefore be double damned: swear you
are chaste!

Desdemona   Heaven truly knows I am.

Othello   Heaven truly knows you are as deceitful as
hell!

Desdemona   To whom, my lord? With whom? How
am I deceitful?

Othello   Oh, Desdemona! [*He pushes her away*]
Away, away, away!

Desdemona   Oh grief! Why are you crying? Am I the
reason for these tears, my lord? If you suspect my
father is behind your recall, don't take it out on me.
If he's your enemy, he's mine too.

Othello   Had it pleased heaven
60   To try me with affliction, had they rained
        All kind of sores and shames on my bare head,
        Steeped me in poverty to the very lips,
        Given to captivity me and my utmost hopes,
        I should have found in some place of my soul
65   A drop of patience. But alas, to make me
        A fixed figure for the time of scorn
        To point his slow unmoving finger at!
        Yet could I bear that too, well, very well;
        But there where I have garnered up my heart,
70   Where either I must live, or bear no life,
        The fountain from the which my current runs,
        Or else dries up: to be discarded thence,
        Or keep it as a cistern for foul toads
        To knot and gender in! Turn thy complexion there,
75   Patience, thou young and rose-lipped cherubin,
        I here look grim as hell!

Desdemona   I hope my noble lord esteems me honest.

Othello   Oh ay! As summer flies are in the shambles,
        That quicken even with blowing.
80   Oh, thou weed, that art so lovely fair,
        And smell'st so sweet that the sense aches at thee.
        Would thou hadst ne'er been born!

Desdemona   Alas, what ignorant sin have I committed?

Othello   Was this fair paper, this most goodly book,
85   Made to write 'whore' upon? What committed?
        Committed? Oh, thou public commoner!
        I should make very forges of my cheeks,
        That would to cinders burn up modesty,
        Did I but speak thy deeds. What committed?
90   Heaven stops the nose at it, and the moon winks;
        The bawdy wind, that kisses all it meets,

Othello   Had it pleased God to make me suffer; had
He rained all kinds of sores and infamy on my bare
head; plunged me into utter poverty; fettered me
and all my great ambitions – I should have found in
some part of my soul a drop of patience. But, alas!
To make me a standing target for the finger of
scorn to point at! I could even bear that, too; well,
very well. But from that place where I have put my
heart in store; where I must either live, or have no
life at all; the spring from which my life-blood
flows, or otherwise dries up; to be rejected! Or to
allow it to be kept as a tank for foul toads to cluster
and to copulate in! Look there, Patience, you young
and red-lipped angel, and change colour! Yes, look
there as grim as hell!

Desdemona   I hope my noble lord believes I'm
chaste?

Othello   Oh yes! As summer flies are in an abbatoir,
that lay their eggs and breed. Oh, you weed – so
lovely to look at, and so sweet to smell that you
make the senses ache – would you had never been
born!

Desdemona   Alas, what sin have I committed in my
ignorance?

Othello   [*holding her face between his hands*] Was
this lovely piece of paper – this exquisite book –
made for writing 'whore' upon? What have you
committed? Committed? Oh, you common harlot!
I'd have to make furnaces of my cheeks,
incinerating modesty, if I were to describe your
deeds! What have you committed? Heaven baulks
at the smell of it, and the chaste moon shuts her
eyes; the promiscuous wind, that kisses all it meets,

Is hushed within the hollow mine of earth
And will not hear it. What committed?
Impudent strumpet!

95 **Desdemona**   By heaven, you do me wrong.

Othello   Are you not a strumpet?

Desdemona   No, as I am a Christian:
If to preserve this vessel for my lord
From any other foul unlawful touch,
100 Be not to be a strumpet, I am none.

Othello   What, not a whore?

Desdemona   No, as I shall be saved.

Othello   Is't possible?

Desdemona   Oh, heaven forgive us!

105 **Othello**   I cry you mercy:
I took you for that cunning whore of Venice
That married with Othello. [*Calling*] You, mistress,
That have the office opposite to Saint Peter
And keep the gate of hell!

[*Enter* **Emilia**]

110   You, you, ay, you!
We have done our course. There's money for your pains.
I pray you turn the key, and keep our counsel.

[*Exit*]

Emilia   Alas, what does this gentleman conceive?
How do you, madam? How do you, my good lady?

115 **Desdemona**   Faith, half asleep.

Emilia   Good madam, what's the matter with my lord?

is silenced in its subterranean cave and refuses to hear about it. What have you committed? You impudent strumpet!

Desdemona   By heaven, you wrong me!

Othello   Are you not a strumpet?

Desdemona   No, as I am a Christian. If not being a strumpet means keeping myself untainted in order to preserve myself for my lord, then I'm not one.

Othello   What! Not a whore?

Desdemona   No, as I hope to be saved.

Othello   Can it be possible?

Desdemona   Oh, God forgive us!

Othello   I beg your pardon, then. I took you for that cunning whore of Venice who married Othello. [*He calls*] You, madam, with the opposite job to St Peter's: keeper of the gate of hell!

[**Emilia** *enters*]

You, you, yes, you! We've finished now. Here's your tip. Lock up, and mum's the word!

[*He goes*]

Emilia   Alas, what is this gentleman thinking of? How are you, madam? How are you, your ladyship?

Desdemona   [*stunned*] Indeed, half asleep.

Emilia   Good madam, what's the matter with my lord?

221

Desdemona   With who?

Emilia   Why, with my lord, madam.

Desdemona   Who is thy lord?

120 **Emilia**   He that is yours, sweet lady.

Desdemona   I have none. Do not talk to me, Emilia.
    I cannot weep; nor answer have I none,
    But what should go by water. Prithee, tonight
    Lay on my bed our wedding sheets, remember,
125   And call thy husband hither.

Emilia   Here is a change indeed!

[*Exit*]

Desdemona   'Tis meet I should be used so, very meet.
    How have I been behaved, that he might stick
    The smallest opinion on my greatest abuse?

[*Enter* **Iago** *and* **Emilia**]

130 **Iago**   What is your pleasure, madam? How is't with you?

Desdemona   I cannot tell: those that do teach young
        babes
    Do it with gentle means and easy tasks;
    He might have chid me so, for, in good faith,
135   I am a child at chiding.

Iago   What is the matter, lady?

Emilia   Alas, Iago, my lord hath so bewhored her,
    Thrown such despite and heavy terms upon her,
    As true heart cannot bear.

140 **Desdemona**   Am I that name, Iago?

Iago   What name, fair lady?

Desdemona   With whom?

Emilia   Why, with my lord, madam.

Desdemona   Who is your lord?

Emilia   Your husband, sweet lady.

Desdemona   I have none. Do not talk to me, Emilia. I cannot weep, nor have I any answers, except those conveyed by tears. Tonight please put our wedding sheets on my bed. Don't forget. And call your husband here.

Emilia   Here's a change indeed!

[*She goes*]

Desdemona   [*ironically*] It's right I should be treated like this; quite right . . . [*Bewildered*] Whatever have I done that he should rebuke me in the slightest even for the worst of my trespasses?

[**Emilia** *enters with* **Iago**]

Iago   What can I do for you, madam? How are you?

Desdemona   I don't know. Those who teach young babies do so gently and with easy tasks. He might have told me off like that, because really, I'm not used to being scolded.

Iago   What is the matter, lady?

Emilia   Alas, Iago, my lord has called her a whore so often; hurled such abuse and hard words at her, that no loyal heart could bear it.

Desdemona   Am I that name, Iago?

Iago   What name, fair lady?

Desdemona   Such as she said my lord did say I was.

Emilia   He called her whore: a beggar in his drink
Could not have laid such terms upon his callat.

145 **Iago**   Why did he so?

Desdemona   I do not know. I am sure I am none such.

Iago   Do not weep, do not weep. Alas the day!

Emilia   Hath she forsook so many noble matches,
Her father, and her country, all her friends,
150 To be called whore? Would it not make one weep?

Desdemona   It is my wretched fortune.

Iago   Beshrew him for it!
How comes this trick upon him?

Desdemona   Nay, heaven doth know.

155 **Emilia**   I will be hanged if some eternal villain,
Some busy and insinuating rogue,
Some cogging cozening slave, to get some office,
Have not devised this slander! I'll be hanged else.

Iago   Fie, there is no such man! It is impossible.

160 **Desdemona**   If any such there be, heaven pardon him.

Emilia   A halter pardon him and hell gnaw his bones!
Why should he call her whore? Who keeps her company?
What place, what time, what form, what likelihood?
The Moor's abused by some most villainous knave,
165 Some base notorious knave, some scurvy fellow.
Oh heaven, that such companions thou'dst unfold,
And put in every honest hand a whip
To lash the rascals naked through the world,
Even from the east to the west!

Desdemona   The one she said my lord said I was.

Emilia   He called her a whore. A drunken beggar wouldn't have said such things about his slut.

Iago   Why did he say that?

Desdemona   I don't know. I'm sure I'm no such thing.

[*She bursts into tears again*]

Iago   Don't cry, don't cry. Oh dear!

Emilia   Has she rejected so many noble suitors, her father, and her country – all her friends – just to be called 'whore'? Wouldn't it make you weep?

Desdemona   It's my wretched misfortune.

Iago   Shame on him! What has brought this on?

Desdemona   Heaven only knows.

Emilia   I'm hanged if some stinking villain – some interfering and ingratiating rogue – some cheating, deceitful wretch – hasn't invented this slander to get some promotion! I'll be hanged if he hasn't!

Iago   Tush. There's no such kind of man. It's impossible.

Desdemona   If such a one exists, may heaven pardon him!

Emilia   A noose pardon him, and hell gnaw his bones! Why should he call her a whore? Who's her lover? Where? When? How? What likelihood? The Moor has been duped by some villainous rogue; some rotten no-good rogue; some lousy wretch! Oh, would that God would expose such villains, and put a whip in every honest hand to lash the rascals naked from one side of the earth to the other!

170 **Iago**   Speak within doors.

Emilia   Oh fie upon them! Some such squire he was
   That turned your wit the seamy side without
   And made you to suspect me with the Moor.

Iago   You are a fool, go to.

175 **Desdemona**   Oh good Iago,
   What shall I do to win my lord again?
   Good friend, go to him; for, by this light of heaven,
   I know not how I lost him. Here I kneel:
   If e'er my will did trespass 'gainst his love,
180   Either in discourse of thought or actual deed;
   Or that mine eyes, mine ears, or any sense
   Delighted them in any other form,
   Or that I do not yet, and ever did,
   And ever will – though he do shake me off
185   To beggarly divorcement – love him dearly,
   Comfort forswear me! Unkindness may do much,
   And his unkindness may defeat my life,
   But never taint my love. I cannot say 'whore':
   It does abhor me now I speak the word;
190   To do the act that might the addition earn
   Not the world's mass of vanity could make me.

   Iago   I pray you, be content: 'tis but his humour,
   The business of the state does him offence,
   And he does chide with you.

195 **Desdemona**   If 'twere no other –

   Iago   It is but so, I warrant you.
   Hark how these instruments summon to supper!
   The messengers of Venice stay the meat.
   Go in, and weep not. All things shall be well.

                              [*Exeunt* **Desdemona** *and* **Emilia**]

Iago Lower your voice.

Emilia Shame on him! It must have been some such joker as the one that brought your nasty side out, and made you think I was having an affair with the Moor!

Iago You are a fool. Be quiet!

Desdemona Oh, good Iago, what shall I do to get my husband back? Good friend, go to him: I swear I don't know how I lost him. [*She falls on her knees*] Here I kneel. If ever I betrayed his love, either mentally or physically; or if ever my eyes, my ears, or any of my senses took delight in anyone but him; or if I do not now, and always did, and always shall, love him dearly – even if he divorces me and I'm in poverty – may I never know happiness again! Unkindness can do much, and his unkindness may be the end of me. But it will never affect my love. I cannot say 'whore'. It disgusts me just to utter the word. Nothing in the wide world could tempt me to do what's required to earn that title.

Iago Don't be upset. It's just his temperament. State business has angered him and he's taking it out on you.

Desdemona If that was all . . .

Iago It is, I'm certain. [*The sound of trumpets is heard*] Listen – it's the call to supper. The Venetian messengers are waiting to dine. Go in, and don't cry. All will be well.

[**Desdemona** *and* **Emilia** *leave*]

[*Enter* **Roderigo**]

200   How now, Roderigo?

Roderigo   I do not find that thou deal'st justly with me.

Iago   What in the contrary?

Roderigo   Every day thou dafts me with some device,
Iago, and rather, as it seems to me, thou keepst from me
205   all conveniency, than suppliest me with the least
advantage of hope. I will indeed no longer endure it.
Nor am I yet persuaded to put up in peace what already
I have foolishly suffered.

Iago   Will you hear me, Roderigo?

210 **Roderigo**   Faith, I have heard too much, for your words
and performances are no kin together.

Iago   You charge me most unjustly.

Roderigo   With naught but truth. I have wasted myself
out of my means. The jewels you have had from me, to
215   deliver to Desdemona, would half have corrupted a
votarist. You have told me she hath received them, and
returned me expectations and comforts of sudden respect
and acquaintance, but I find none.

Iago   Well, go to, very well.

220 **Roderigo**   Very well, go to! I cannot go to, man, nor 'tis
not very well. I say it is very scurvy and begin to find
myself fopped in it.

Iago   Very well.

Roderigo   I tell you it is not very well. I will make myself
225   known to Desdemona. If she will return me my jewels, I
will give over my suit and repent my unlawful
solicitation. If not, assure yourself I will seek satisfaction
of you.

[**Roderigo** *enters*]

Well, Roderigo?

Roderigo You're not playing fair with me!

Iago Whyever not?

Roderigo Every day you put me off with some excuse, Iago. It seems to me you thwart me rather than give me the slightest hope. I'll put up with it no longer. And I'm not inclined to overlook what I've already foolishly suffered.

Iago Will you listen to me, Roderigo?

Roderigo 'Strewth, I've listened too much. What you say and what you do are two different things.

Iago That's most unjust!

Roderigo It's true. I'm bankrupt. The jewels I gave you to give to Desdemona would have been more than enough to corrupt a nun. You've told me she's received them, and in return indicated that my hopes will soon be realised: but nothing has happened.

Iago Well, get stuck in. All right?

Roderigo All right indeed! I can't get stuck in, man, and it's not all right! I think it's all rotten, and I'm beginning to think I've been taken in.

Iago All right.

Roderigo I tell you it isn't all right. I'll make myself known to Desdemona. If she'll give me my jewels back, I'll withdraw as her suitor and apologize for my improper advances. If not, be assured I'll seek revenge!

Iago   You have said now.

230 **Roderigo**   Ay, and said nothing but what I protest intendment of doing.

Iago   Why, now I see there's mettle in thee; and even from this time do build on thee a better opinion than ever before. Give me thy hand, Roderigo. Thou hast taken
235   against me a most just exception, but yet I protest I have dealt most directly in thy affairs.

Roderigo   It hath not appeared.

Iago   I grant indeed it hath not appeared, and your suspicion is not without wit and judgement. But,
240   Roderigo, if thou hast that in thee indeed, which I have greater reason to believe now than ever – I would mean purpose, courage, and valour – this night show it. If thou the next night following enjoy not Desdemona, take me from this world with treachery, and devise engines
245   for my life.

Roderigo   Well, is it within reason and compass?

Iago   Sir, there is especial commission come from Venice to depute Cassio to Othello's place.

Roderigo   Is that true? Why, then Othello and Desdemona
250   return again to Venice.

Iago   Oh, no: he goes into Mauritania, and takes away with him the fair Desdemona, unless his abode be lingered here by some accident; wherein none can be so determinate as the removing of Cassio.

255 **Roderigo**   How do you mean 'removing' of him?

Iago   Why, by making him uncapable of Othello's place – knocking out his brains.

Roderigo   And that you would have me to do?

Iago That's talking!

Roderigo Yes, and I've said nothing I don't intend to carry out.

Iago Well, now I see you've got guts! My opinion of you has risen. Give me your hand, Roderigo. You've made a very good point against me, but I insist I've done my honest best for you.

Roderigo I haven't noticed it.

Iago I admit there's not much sign of it, and your suspicion is not without common sense and intelligence. However, Roderigo, if you indeed have in you what I've greater reason than ever to believe is there – I mean determination, courage, and valour – demonstrate it this very night. If the following night you don't sleep with Desdemona, make your plans and do me in.

Roderigo Well, is it wise and prudent?

Iago Sir, a special delegation has come from Venice to appoint Cassio in Othello's place.

Roderigo Is that so? Why then, Othello and Desdemona will go back to Venice.

Iago Oh, no. He's going on to Mauritania, taking with him the beautiful Desdemona, unless he's kept here by some accident. Nothing could be more appropriate than the removing of Cassio.

Roderigo How do you mean – 'removing' him?

Iago Why, by making him incapable of taking Othello's place. Bashing his brains out.

Roderigo And that's what you want me to do?

Iago   Ay, if you dare do yourself a profit and a right. He
260   sups tonight with a harlot, and thither will I go to him.
He knows not yet of his honourable fortune. If you will
watch his going thence, which I will fashion to fall out
between twelve and one, you may take him at your
pleasure. I will be near to second your attempt, and he
265   shall fall between us. Come, stand not amazed at it, but
go along with me. I will show you such a necessity in his
death that you shall think yourself bound to put it on
him. It is now high supper-time and the night grows to
waste. About it!

270   **Roderigo**   I will hear further reason for this.

Iago   And you shall be satisfied.

[*Exeunt*]

Scene 3

Cyprus. Another room in the Castle. Enter **Othello, Lodovico,
Desdemona, Emilia,** *and attendants.*

Lodovico   I do beseech you, sir, trouble yourself no
further.

Othello   Oh, pardon me: it shall do me good to walk.

Lodovico   Madam, good night. I humbly thank your
5   ladyship.

Desdemona   Your honour is most welcome.

Othello   Will you walk, sir? Oh, Desdemona!

Desdemona   My lord?

Iago   Yes, if you dare do yourself a favour, and a right. He's dining tonight with some floozie. I'll go to him there. He doesn't yet know about his promotion. If you look out for his departure – which I'll arrange to be between twelve o'clock and one – you can take him at your pleasure. I'll be nearby to second you, so between us he's done for. Don't look so surprised; come along with me. I'll give you such convincing reasons for his death that you'll feel compelled to do him in. It's supper-time already and the night is going to waste. Get going!

Roderigo   I need more persuading.

Iago   You'll be convinced.

   [*They go*]

Scene 3

Othello, Lodovico, Desdemona, Emilia *and Attendants enter.*

Lodovico   Please, trouble yourself no further, sir.

Othello   Not at all. It will do me good to walk.

Lodovico   Madam, good night. My respectful thanks to your ladyship.

Desdemona   Your honour is most welcome.

Othello   Are you ready, sir? Desdemona –

Desdemona   My lord?

Othello   Get you to bed on the instant. I will be returned
10   forthwith. Dispatch your attendant there. Look it be
done.

Desdemona   I will, my lord.

[*Exeunt* **Othello, Lodovico,** *and Attendants*]

Emilia   How goes it now? He looks gentler than he did.

Desdemona   He says he will return incontinent.
15   He hath commanded me to go to bed,
And bade me to dismiss you.

Emilia   Dismiss me?

Desdemona   It was his bidding, Therefore, good Emilia,
Give me my nightly wearing, and adieu.
20   We must not now displease him.

Emilia   I would you had never seen him!   *never met him*

Desdemona   So would not I. My love doth so approve him
That even his stubbornness, his checks, his frowns –   *admirable qualities & speaks about him very nice?*
Prithee, unpin me – have grace and favour in them.

25 **Emilia**   I have laid those sheets you bade me on the bed.

Desdemona   All's one. Good faith, how foolish are our
minds!
If I do die before thee, prithee shroud me   *put wedding sheets on re kindle feeling when they spent time t*
In one of those same sheets.

30 **Emilia**   Come, come, you talk.

Desdemona   My mother had a maid called Barbary:
She was in love and he she loved proved mad   *very bleak response*
And did forsake her. She had a song of willow;
An old thing 'twas; but it expressed her fortune,
35   And she died singing it. That song tonight
Will not go from my mind. I have much to do

234

Othello   Go to bed at once. I'll be back soon. Dismiss your maidservant. See to it.

Desdemona   I will, my lord.

[**Othello, Lodovico** *and Attendants leave*]

Emilia   How goes it now? He looks gentler than he did.

Desdemona   He says he will return immediately. He has ordered me to go to bed, and told me to send you away.

Emilia   Send me away?

Desdemona   Those were his orders. Therefore, good Emilia, give me my night clothes, and farewell. We mustn't displease him now.

Emilia   I wish you had never seen him! [*She busies herself with her tasks*]

Desdemona   I don't. I love him so much that even his stubbornness, his harsh words and his frowns – please, unpin me – have attractiveness and charm.

Emilia   [*undoing* **Desdemona's** *hair*] I've laid those sheets on the bed, as you told me.

Desdemona   All right. Really, how foolish our thoughts can be! Should I die before you, shroud me in one of those sheets.

Emilia   How you do go on!

Desdemona   My mother had a maid called Barbary. She was in love. The man she loved turned out to be unfaithful, and left her. She had a song about a willow. An old one it was, but it fitted her situation and she died singing it. I can't get that song out of

But to go hang my head all at one side,
And sing it like poor Barbary. Prithee, dispatch.

Emilia   Shall I go fetch your night-gown?

40 **Desdemona**   No, unpin me here.
This Lodovico is a proper man.

Emilia   A very handsome man.

Desdemona   He speaks well.

Emilia   I know a lady in Venice would have walked
45   barefoot to Palestine for a touch of his nether lip.

Desdemona   [*sings*]
   The poor soul sat sighing by a sycamore tree,
      Sing all a green willow;
   Her hand on her bosom, her head on her knee,
50   *Sing willow, willow, willow;*
   The fresh streams ran by her and murmured her moans;
      Sing willow, willow, willow;
   Her salt tears fell from her and softened the stones –
   Lay by these.
55   [*sings*] *Sing willow, willow, willow –*
   Prithee hie thee; he'll come anon.
   [*Sings*]   *Sing all a green willow must be my garland.*
   Let nobody blame him; his scorn I approve –
   Nay, that's not next. Hark, who is't that knocks?

60 **Emilia**   It's the wind.

my mind tonight. I'm tempted to hang my head on one side and sing it like poor Barbary. Please hurry!

Emilia   Shall I go fetch your nightgown?

Desdemona   No. Undo this pin here. That Lodovico is a nice man.

Emilia   A very handsome man.

Desdemona   He speaks well.

Emilia   I know a lady in Venice who would walk barefoot to Palestine for one of his kisses.

Desdemona   [*singing*]
The poor soul sat sighing by a sycamore tree,
  Sing all-a-green willow,
Her hand on her bosom, her head on her knee,
  Sing willow, willow, willow.
The fresh streams ran by her, and murmured her moans;
  Sing willow, willow, willow.
Her salt tears fell from her which softened the stones —

[*To* **Emilia**, *speaking and handing her some jewels*]

Put these over there.

[*resuming her song*] *Sing, willow, willow, willow—*

[*speaking again*] Hurry. He'll be here soon.

[*singing*] *Sing all-a-green willow must be my garland.*
Let nobody blame him; his scorn I approve—

[*speaking*] No, that's not the next line. [*She pauses, listening*] Listen. Who's that knocking?

Emilia   It's the wind.

Desdemona   [*sings*]
  I called my love false love, but what said he then?
    Sing willow, willow, willow:
  If I court moe women, you'll couch with moe men.
65 Now get thee gone. Good night. Mine eyes do itch:
  Does that bode weeping?

Emilia   'Tis neither here nor there.

Desdemona   I have heard it said so, Oh, these men, these
  men!
70 Dost thou in conscience think – tell me, Emilia –
  That there be women do abuse their husbands
  In such gross kind?

Emilia   There be some such, no question.

Desdemona   Wouldst thou do such a deed, for all the
75 world?

Emilia   Why, would not you?

Desdemona   No, by this heavenly light!

Emilia   Nor I neither by this heavenly light; I might do it
  as well in the dark.

80 **Desdemona**   Wouldst thou do such a deed for all the
  world?

Emilia   The world is a huge thing. It is a great price for a
  small vice.

Desdemona   In troth, I think thou wouldst not.

85 **Emilia**   In troth I think I should, and undo't when I had
  done it. Marry, I would not do such a thing for a joint
  ring, nor for measures of lawn, nor for gowns, petticoats,
  nor caps, nor any such exhibition. But for the whole
  world? Ud's pity, who would not make her husband a
90 cuckold, to make him a monarch? I should venture
  purgatory for it.

Desdemona   [*singing*]
I called my love false love, but what said he then?
  Sing willow, willow, willow.
If I court more women, you'll sleep with more men.

[*speaking*] Go now. Good night. My eyes are
itching. Does that foretell weeping?

Emilia   Neither one thing nor the other.

Desdemona   That's what I've heard. Oh, these men,
these men! Do you honestly think – tell me,
Emilia! – that there are women who cheat their
husbands in that disgusting way?

Emilia   Some do, without a doubt.

Desdemona   Would you do such a thing, for anything
in the world?

Emilia   Why – wouldn't you?

Desdemona   No, by the light of the sun!

Emilia   I wouldn't either, by light of the sun . . . I
might do it in the dark, though.

Desdemona   Would you do such a thing for all the
world?

Emilia   The world's a huge thing. It's a lot to sacrifice
for a small sin.

Desdemona   Truly, I don't think you would.

Emilia   Truly, I think I should, and then wish I hadn't
afterwards. Well, I wouldn't do such a thing for a
fancy ring, or for rolls of linen, or gowns, petticoats,
hats or any trifle. But for the whole world? For
God's sake, who wouldn't deceive her husband to
make him a king? I'd risk purgatory for that.

Desdemona   Beshrew me, if I would do such a wrong for
the whole world!

Emilia   Why, the wrong is but a wrong in the world; and
95   having the world for your labour, 'tis a wrong in your
own world, and you might quickly make it right.

Desdemona   I do not think there is any such woman.

Emilia   Yes, a dozen: and as many to the vantage as
would store the world they played for.
100   But I do think it is their husbands' faults
If wives do fall. Say that they slack their duties,
And pour our treasures into foreign laps;
Or else break out in peevish jealousies,
Throwing restraint upon us; or say they strike us,
105   Or scant our former having in despite:
Why, we have galls; and though we have some grace,
Yet we have some revenge. Let husbands know:
Their wives have sense like them: they see and smell,
And have their palates both for sweet and sour
110   As husbands have. What is it that they do,
When they change us for others? Is it sport?
I think it is. And doth affection breed it?
I think it doth. Is't frailty that thus errs?
It is so too. And have not we affections,
115   Desires for sport, and frailty, as men have?
Then let them use us well: else let them know
The ills we do, their ills instruct us so.

Desdemona   Good night, good night. God me such usage
send,
120   Not to pick bad from bad, but by bad mend!

[*Exeunt*]

Desdemona   I wouldn't do such a wrong for the whole world, believe me!

Emilia   Why, the wrong is only a worldly wrong; and if you had the world as your reward, it's a wrong in the world that you own, so you could quickly put it right!

Desdemona   I don't think there is any such woman.

Emilia   Yes, a dozen; and as many in addition as would populate the world they were out to get. I think it's the husbands' fault if wives go off the rails. If they neglect us and have a bit on the side; or break out into peevish jealousy, and restrict our liberty; or hit us, or keep us short of housekeeping money out of spite: why, we have spirit, and though we have gentleness, we also have the ability to revenge. Let husbands know that their wives have feelings as they do. They see and smell, and have a taste for both sweet and sour just as their husbands have. What makes them change us for others? Is it for amusement? I think it is. And does passion cause it? I think it does. Is it human weakness that is therefore at fault? It certainly is. And haven't we got passions, desire for amusement, and human weakness like men have? So they'd better treat us well – or else let them know that we only play the games they teach us

Desdemona   Goodnight, goodnight. May God make me learn from the bad, not copy them!

[*They go*]

Act five

Scene 1

Cyprus. A street. Enter **Iago** *and* **Roderigo**.

Iago   Here stand behind this bulk; straight will he come.
Wear thy good rapier bare, and put it home.
Quick, quick; fear nothing: I'll be at thy elbow.
It makes us or it mars us; think on that,
5   And fix most firm thy resolution.

Roderigo   Be near at hand; I may miscarry in't.

Iago   Here, at thy hand: be bold, and take thy stand.

[*He retires*]

Roderigo   I have no great devotion to the deed,
And yet he hath given me satisfying reasons.
10   'Tis but a man gone. Forth my sword! He dies.

Iago   I have rubbed this young quat almost to the sense,
And he grows angry. Now, whether he kill Cassio,
Or Cassio him, or each do kill the other,
Every way makes my game. Live Roderigo,
15   He calls me to a restitution large
Of gold and jewels, that I bobbed from him
As gifts to Desdemona.
It must not be. If Cassio do remain
He hath a daily beauty in his life
20   That makes me ugly; and besides, the Moor
May unfold me to him. There I stand in much peril.
No, he must die. Be't so. I hear him coming.

[*Enter* **Cassio**]

Act five

Scene 1

A street in Cyprus. Enter **Iago** *and* **Roderigo**.

Iago Here, stand behind this shopfront. He'll be here soon. Draw your sword, and drive it home. Quick, quick! Don't be afraid. I'll be at your elbow. This makes us or breaks us. Think about that, and be resolute!

Roderigo Be near at hand. I may botch it.

Iago Here, at your side. Be brave, and take up your position.

[**Iago** *stands back*]

Roderigo I've no great love for this deed, but he's given me very sound reasons. It's only one man less. Out with my sword. He dies!

Iago I've touched a raw nerve in this young wart, and he's angry. Now, whether he kills Cassio, or Cassio kills him, or they both get killed, I can't lose. If Roderigo lives, he'll want the load of gold and jewels back that I screwed out of him as gifts to Desdemona. No way! If Cassio survives, his popularity and charm will make me look ugly. Besides, the Moor may denounce me to him. There I'm in great danger. No – he must die. Right, then – I can hear him coming.

[**Cassio** *enters*]

Roderigo   I know his gait; 'tis he. Villain, thou diest!

Cassio   That thrust had been mine enemy indeed,
25   But that my coat is better than thou think'st.
I will make proof of thine. — *challenges him*

[*He wounds* **Roderigo**]

Roderigo   Oh, I am slain!

[**Iago** *wounds* **Cassio** *in the leg, and exits*]

Cassio   I am maimed for ever. Help, ho! Murder, murder!

[*Enter* **Othello**]

Othello   The voice of Cassio: Iago keeps his word.

30 **Roderigo**   Oh, villain that I am!

Othello   It is even so.

Cassio   Oh, help, ho! Light! A surgeon!

Othello   'Tis he! Oh brave Iago, honest and just,
That hast such noble sense of thy friend's wrong,
35   Thou teachest me! Minion, your dear lies dead,
And your fate hies apace. Strumpet, I come!
Forth of my heart those charms, thine eyes, are blotted;
Thy bed, lust-stained, shall with lust's blood be spotted.

[*Exit* **Othello**]

[*Enter* **Lodovico** *and* **Gratiano**]

Cassio   What, ho! No watch? No passage? Murder,
40   murder!

Roderigo   I know his walk. It's him. [*He jumps out*]
Villain, you're dead!

Cassio   That thrust would have killed me for sure, but
my jerkin is tougher than you think. I'll see what
yours is like!

[*He draws his sword and wounds* **Roderigo**]

Roderigo   Oh, I've been killed!

[**Iago** *steps forward, wounds* **Cassio** *in the leg, then
runs off*]

Cassio   I'm maimed for life! Help, ho! Murder,
murder!

[**Othello** *appears at the window above*]

Othello   Cassio's voice. Iago is keeping his word.

Roderigo   Oh, I'm a villain!

Othello   [*thinking he hears* **Cassio**] Indeed so.

Cassio   Oh, help, ho! Some light! A surgeon!

Othello   That's him! Oh, brave Iago, honest and just!
You have such noble understanding of the wrong
done to your friend, you set me an example! Hussy,
your lover is dead, and your time nigh! Strumpet,
I'm coming! Those charms, your eyes, no longer
move my heart. Your bed, lust-stained, will soon be
spotted with lust's blood!

[**Othello** *goes*]

[**Lodovico** *and* **Gratiano** *enter*]

Cassio   Help! Is there nobody on watch! No passers-
by? Murder, murder!

Gratiano   'Tis some mischance. The cry is very direful.

Cassio   Oh, help!

Lodovico   Hark!

Roderigo   Oh wretched villain!

45 **Lodovico**   Two or three groan. It is a heavy night.
These may be counterfeits. Let's think't unsafe
To come into the cry without more help.

Roderigo   Nobody come? Then shall I bleed to death.

Lodovico   Hark!

[*Enter* **Iago**, *with a light*]

50 **Gratiano**   Here's one comes in his shirt, with light and
weapons.

Iago   Who's there? Whose noise is this that cries on
murder?

Lodovico   I do not know.

55 **Iago**   Did you not hear a cry?

Cassio   Here, here: for heaven's sake help me!

Iago   What's the matter?

Gratiano   This is Othello's Ancient, as I take it.

Lodovico   The same indeed, a very valiant fellow.

60 **Iago**   What are you here, that cry so grievously?

Cassio   Iago? Oh, I am spoiled, undone by villains!
Give me some help.

Iago   Oh my Lieutenant! What villains have done this?

Gratiano   Something's wrong. That was a cry of distress!

Cassio   Oh, help!

Lodovico   Listen!

Roderigo   Oh, wretched villain!

Lodovico   Two or three groans. It's a dark night. They may be decoys. Don't let's get involved without more help.

Roderigo   Is nobody coming? I'll bleed to death.

Lodovico   Listen!

[**Iago** *enters with a light*]

Gratiano   Here's someone in his nightshirt, with a light and weapons.

Iago   Who's there? Who's calling 'murder'?

Lodovico   I don't know.

Iago   Didn't you hear a cry?

Cassio   Here, here, for heaven's sake, help me!

Iago   What's the matter?

Gratiano   This is Othello's Staff-Sergeant, I think.

Lodovico   It is indeed. A very valiant fellow.

Iago   Who's here, shouting in distress?

Cassio   Iago? Oh, I'm killed: done for by villains! Help me!

Iago   Oh, Lieutenant! What rogues did this?

Cassio I think that one of them is hereabout
65   And cannot make away.

Iago   Oh treacherous villains!
What are you there? Come in and give some help.

Roderigo Oh, help me here!

Cassio That's one of them.

70 **Iago**   Oh murd'rous slave! Oh villain!

[*He stabs* **Roderigo**]

Roderigo Oh damned Iago! Oh inhuman dog!

[*He faints*]

Iago Kill him i'the dark? Where be these bloody thieves?
How silent is this town! Ho, murder, murder!

[**Lodovico** *and* **Gratiano** *come forward*]

What may you be? Are you of good or evil?

75 **Lodovico** As you shall prove us, praise us.

Iago Signor Lodovico?

Lodovico He, sir.

Iago I cry you mercy. Here's Cassio hurt by villains.

Gratiano Cassio?

80 **Iago** How is it, brother?

Cassio My leg is cut in two.

Cassio   I think one of them is somewhere near, and can't get away.

Iago   Oh, you treacherous villains! [*seeing* **Lodovico** *and* **Gratiano**] Who's there? Come nearer and give some help.

Roderigo   Oh, help me here!

Cassio   That's one of them.

Iago   You murderous wretch! You villain!

[*He stabs* **Roderigo**]

Roderigo   Oh, damned Iago! You inhuman dog!

[*He faints*]

Iago   Kill him in the dark? Where are these bloodthirsty thieves? How quiet the town is! Ho, Murder, murder!

[**Lodovico** *and* **Gratiano** *come forward*]

Who are you? What are you – friend or foe?

Lodovico   Take us as you find us.

Iago   Signor Lodovico?

Lodovico   That's me.

Iago   I beg your pardon. Here's Cassio. He's been hurt by villains.

Gratiano   Cassio?

Iago   How are you, brother?

Cassio   My leg's been cut in two.

Act five   Scene 1

Iago   Marry, heaven forbid!
   Light, gentlemen. I'll bind it with my shirt.

   [*Enter* **Bianca**]

Bianca   What is the matter, ho? Who is't that cried?

85 **Iago**   Who is't that cried?

Bianca   Oh, my dear Cassio, my sweet Cassio!
   Oh, Cassio, Cassio, Cassio!

Iago   Oh notable strumpet! Cassio, may you suspect
   Who they should be, that have thus mangled you?

90 **Cassio**   No.

Gratiano   I am sorry to find you thus, I have been to seek
   you.

Iago   Lend me a garter: so. Oh for a chair
   To bear him easily hence!

95 **Bianca**   Alas, he faints!
   Oh Cassio, Cassio, Cassio!

Iago   Gentlemen all, I do suspect this trash
   To bear a part in this.
   Patience awhile, good Cassio. Come, come,
100 Lend me a light. Know we this face or no?
   Alas, my friend, and my dear countryman
   Roderigo? No – yes, sure – Oh heaven, Roderigo!

Gratiano   What, of Venice?

Iago   Even he, sir. Did you know him?

105 **Gratiano**   Know him! Ay.

Iago   Oh, God forbid! Some light, gentlemen. [*They bring their torches so that* **Iago** *can see the wound*] I'll bind it with my shirt.

[**Bianca** *enters*]

Bianca   What's the matter there, hey? Who called?

Iago   Who called?

Bianca   [*seeing* **Cassio's** *distress*] Oh, my dear Cassio, my sweet Cassio! Oh, Cassio, Cassio, Cassio! [*She holds him in her arms*]

Iago   Infamous strumpet! Cassio, have you any idea who wounded you?

Cassio   No.

Gratiano   I'm sorry to find you like this. I've been looking for you.

Iago   [*hastily interrupting*] Lend me a garter. [*He uses it as a tourniquet*] I wish we had a chair to carry him away in comfort.

Bianca   Oh, he's fainted! Oh, Cassio, Cassio, Cassio!

Iago   Gentlemen, I suspect this trollop had a hand in this. Be patient a little longer, Cassio; come, come. (*To* **Lodovico**) Lend me a light. [*He inspects the body of* **Roderigo**] Do we know this face? [*He acts out shock and surprise*] Roderigo? No. Yes, it is! Oh God! Roderigo!

Gratiano   What, the Venetian?

Iago   The very one sir. Did you know him?

Gratiano   Know him? Yes.

Iago   Signor Gratiano, I cry you gentle pardon.
These bloody accidents must excuse my manners
That so neglected you.

Gratiano   I am glad to see you.

110 **Iago**   How do you, Cassio? Oh, a chair, a chair!

Gratiano   Roderigo!

Iago   He, 'tis he.

[*A chair is brought in*]

                              Oh that's well said, a chair!
Some good man bear him carefully from hence.
115   I'll fetch the General's surgeon. [*To* **Bianca**] For you,
        mistress,
Save you your labour. He that lies slain here, Cassio,
Was my dear friend. What malice was between you?

Cassio   None in the world, nor do I know the man.
120 **Iago**   [*to* **Bianca**] What, look you pale? Oh, bear him out
o'the air.

[**Cassio** *and* **Roderigo** *are borne off*]

Stay you, good gentlewoman. Look you pale, mistress?
Do you perceive the gastness of her eye?
Nay, an you stir – We shall hear more anon.
125   Behold her well; I pray you. Look upon her.
Do you see, gentlemen? Nay, guiltiness will speak
Though tongues were out of use.

[*Enter* **Emilia**]

Emilia   'Las, what's the matter? What's the matter,
husband?

Iago   Signor Gratiano? My apologies. All this bloodshed must excuse my ill manners in overlooking you.

Gratiano   I'm glad to see you.

Iago   How are you, Cassio? Oh, a chair, a chair!

Gratiano   [*inspecting the body himself*] Roderigo!

Iago   Yes, him. It's him.

[*Attendants bring in a chair*]

Oh, well done. A chair! Some good fellow carry him carefully away. I'll fetch the General's surgeon. [*To* **Bianca**, *who is comforting* **Cassio**] As for you, madam, you can save yourself the trouble. The man who lies wounded here was my friend, Cassio. [*To* **Cassio**] What was the quarrel about?

Cassio   There wasn't one. I don't know the man, either.

Iago   [*To* **Bianca**] What, are you turning pale? [*To Attendants*] Carry him indoors. [**Cassio** *is taken into the house.* **Roderigo's** *body is removed*] If you'd stay, good gentleman. [*To* **Bianca**] Stay where you are, my lady. Looking pale, madam? [*To* **Lodovico** *and* **Gratiano**] Do you see how frightened she looks? [*To* **Bianca**, *warningly.*] Don't move . . . we'll hear more about this later. [*To* **Lodovico** *and* **Gratiano**] Take a good look at her. Look at her, will you? Do you see, gentlemen? Yes, guilt will speak out even if tongues go out of use!

[**Emilia** *enters*]

Emilia   What's the matter? What's the matter, husband?

130 **Iago**   Cassio has here been set on in the dark
By Roderigo and fellows that are scaped:
He's almost slain and Roderigo dead.

Emilia   Alas, good gentleman! Alas, good Cassio!

Iago   This is the fruit of whoring. Prithee, Emilia,
135 Go know of Cassio where he supped tonight.
What, do you shake at that?

women of
rap with
men

Bianca   He supped at my house, but I therefore shake not.

turns on
Bianca
Married woman

Iago   Oh, did he so? I charge you go with me.

Emilia   Fie, fie upon thee, strumpet!

140 **Bianca**   I am no strumpet, but of life as honest
As you that thus abuse me.

Emilia   As I? Foh! Fie upon that!

Iago   Kind gentleman, let's see poor Cassio dressed. *bandage*
Come, mistress, you must tell's another tale.
Bianca
145 Emilia, run you to the citadel, — *castle*
And tell my lord and lady what has happed.
Will you go on afore? [*Aside*] This is the night
That either makes me, or fordoes me quite.

Cassio dies
+ Des dies
                                      [*Exeunt*]

Dramatise of him saying it
to the audience

Iago   Cassio has been attacked here in the dark by Roderigo and some other fellows who've escaped. He's severely injured. Roderigo is dead.

Emilia   Oh, the poor gentleman! Oh, good Cassio!

Iago   This is what comes of whoring. Emilia, go and ask Cassio where he dined tonight, will you? [*To* **Bianca**] What, does that make you tremble?

Bianca   He dined at my house, but that's no reason to tremble.

Iago   Oh, did he really? I order you to come with me!

Emilia   Oh, shame on you, you strumpet!

Bianca   I'm no strumpet, but as decent-living as any of you loud-mouths!

Emilia   As me? Pah! Shame on you!

Iago   Kind gentlemen, let's see poor Cassio attended to. [*To* **Bianca**] Come, madam, you'd better change your story. Emilia, run to the Castle and tell my lord and lady what has happened. [*To the others*] Will you go on ahead? [*Aside*] This is the night that either makes or breaks me!

[*They go*]

Scene 2

A bedroom in the Castle. Enter **Othello**, *with a light,*
Desdemona *in bed asleep.*

Othello   It is the cause, it is the cause, my soul:
Let me not name it to you, you chaste stars!
It is the cause. Yet I'll not shed her blood,
Nor scar that whiter skin of hers than snow,
5 And smooth as monumental alabaster:
Yet she must die, else she'll betray more men.
Put out the light, and then put out the light;
If I quench thee, thou flaming minister,
I can again thy former light restore,
10 Should I repent me; but once put out thy light,
Thou cunning pattern of excelling nature,
I know not where is that Promethean heat
That can thy light relume. When I have plucked the
rose,
15 I cannot give it vital growth again,
It needs must wither. I'll smell it on the tree.

[*He kisses her*]

A balmy breath, that doth almost persuade
Justice to break her sword! One more, one more.
Be thus when thou art dead and I will kill thee,
20 And love thee after. One more, and this the last.
So sweet was ne'er so fatal. I must weep.
But they are cruel tears; this sorrow's heavenly:
It strikes where it does love. She wakes.

Desdemona   Who's there? Othello?

25 **Othello**   Ay, Desdemona.

Scene 2

The bedroom of **Othello** *and* **Desdemona**. **Desdemona**
*is asleep in a four-poster bed; the curtains round it are
not drawn.* **Othello** *enters, carrying a light.*

Othello   That [*he means adultery*] is the offence; that
is the charge, my soul. Let me spare you its name,
you chaste stars! That is the accusation. But I will
not shed her blood, nor scar her skin, <u>that's whiter
than snow</u> and smooth as sculptural stone. But she
must die, or she'll betray more men. I'll put out this
light [*he means the torch he is carrying*] and then
put out the light [*he means kill* **Desdemona**]. If I
quench you – my torch – I can re-light you if I
change my mind. [*Addressing* **Desdemona**] But if I
once put out you paragon of nature's excellence, I
don't know where to find the divine spark that can
rekindle you. When I have plucked your rose, [*he
means 'taken your life'*] I cannot put it back to grow
again: it has to wither. I'll smell it on the tree. [*He
kisses her as she sleeps*] A sweet breath, that
almost deflects the course of Justice. One more,
one more. [*He kisses her again*] Be as lovely when
you are dead, and I will kill you, and still love you
afterwards. One more, and this the last. [*He kisses
her for the last time*] Never was it so fatal to be so
sweet. [*Tears roll down his cheeks*] I must weep . . .
But they are pitiless tears. This sorrow comes from
heaven – it smites where it loves most. [**Desdemona**
stirs] She wakens!

Desdemona   Who's there? Othello?

Othello   Yes, Desdemona.

Desdemona   Will you come to bed, my lord?

Othello   Have you prayed tonight, Desdemona?

Desdemona   Ay, my lord.

Othello   If you bethink yourself of any crime
30   Unreconciled as yet to heaven and grace,
        Solicit for it straight.

Desdemona   Alas, my lord, what may you mean by that?

Othello   Well, do it, and be brief. I will walk by:
        I would not kill thy unprepared spirit;
35   No – heaven forfend! – I would not kill thy soul.

Desdemona   Talk you of killing?

Othello   Ay, I do.

Desdemona   Then heaven
        Have mercy on me!

40 **Othello**   Amen, with all my heart!

Desdemona   If you say so, I hope you will not kill me.

Othello   Hum!

Desdemona   And yet I fear you: for you are fatal then
        When your eyes roll so. Why I should fear I know not,
45   Since guiltiness I know not; but yet I feel I fear.

Othello   Think on thy sins.

Desdemona   They are loves I bear to you.

Othello   And for that thou diest.

Desdemona   That death's unnatural that kills for loving.
50   Alas, why gnaw you so your nether lip?

258

Desdemona   Will you come to bed, my lord?

Othello   Have you prayed tonight, Desdemona?

Desdemona   Yes, my lord.

Othello   If you can think of any crime not yet confessed and shriven, make your peace now.

Desdemona   Alas, my lord, what do you mean by that?

Othello   Well, do it and be quick. I'll walk aside. I would not kill you with your sins upon you. No – heaven forbid! I would not kill your soul!

Desdemona   Are you talking about killing?

Othello   Yes, I am.

Desdemona   Then heaven have mercy on me!

Othello   Amen, with all my heart.

Desdemona   If you say that, then I hope you will not kill me.

Othello   Hum!

Desdemona   And yet I fear you. When your eyes roll like that, you have a menacing look. I don't know why I should be afraid, since I am guilty of nothing. Nevertheless, I feel frightened.

Othello   Consider your sins.

Desdemona   Only what I've done for love of you.

Othello   Yes. And for that you will die.

Desdemona   It's unnatural to kill someone for loving. Alas, why do you bite your bottom lip like that?

Some bloody passion shakes your very frame:
These are portents; but yet I hope, I hope,
They do not point on me.

Othello   Peace, and be still!

55 **Desdemona**   I will – so. What's the matter?

Othello   That handkerchief which I so loved and gave
    thee,
Thou gavest to Cassio.

Desdemona   No, by my life and soul!
60 Send for the man and ask him.

Othello   Sweet soul, take heed,
Take heed of perjury: thou art on thy death-bed.

Desdemona   Ay, but not yet to die.

Othello   Yes, presently.
65 Therefore confess thee freely of thy sin;
For to deny each article with oath
Cannot remove nor choke the strong conceit
That I do groan withal. Thou art to die.

Desdemona   Then Lord have mercy on me!

70 **Othello**   I say, amen.

Desdemona   And have you mercy too! I never did
Offend you in my life; never loved Cassio
But with such general warranty of heaven
As I might love. I never gave him token.

75 **Othello**   By heaven, I saw my handkerchief in his hand!
Oh perjured woman! Thou dost stone my heart,
And mak'st me call what I intend to do
A murder, which I thought a sacrifice.
I saw the handkerchief.

Your whole body is shaking with some murderous passion. These are ominous signs, but I hope, I hope, they do not point at me!

Othello   Quiet, and be still!

Desdemona   I will. [*She composes herself*] So. What is this all about?

Othello   That handkerchief which I loved so much, and gave to you, you gave to Cassio.

Desdemona   Upon my life and soul I didn't! Send for the man and ask him!

Othello   Sweet soul, take heed. Take heed of perjury. You are on your death-bed.

Desdemona   Yes, but I am not to die yet.

Othello   Yes. Now. Therefore freely confess your sins. Denying everything under oath will neither remove nor suppress the strong conviction that is grieving me. You are to die.

Desdemona   Then lord have mercy on me!

Othello   Amen to that.

Desdemona   And give you mercy, too! I never wronged you in my life: never loved Cassio other than in a proper way. I never gave him a love-token.

Othello   By heaven, I saw my handkerchief in his hand! Oh, you perjured woman! You turn my heart to stone, and make me call what I intend to do a murder, which I thought of as a sacrifice. I saw the handkerchief!

80 **Desdemona**   He found it then.
I never gave it him. Send for him hither.
Let him confess a truth.

Othello   He hath confessed.

Desdemona   What, my lord?

85 **Othello**   That he hath used thee.

Desdemona   How? Unlawfully?

Othello   Ay.

Desdemona   He will not say so.

Othello   No, his mouth is stopped:
90   Honest Iago hath ta'en order for't.

Desdemona   My fear interprets then. What, is he dead?

Othello   Had all his hairs been lives, my great revenge
Had stomach for them all.

Desdemona   Alas, he is betrayed, and I undone.

95 **Othello**   Out, strumpet! Weep'st thou for him to my face!

Desdemona   Oh banish me, my lord, but kill me not!

Othello   Down, strumpet!

Desdemona   Kill me tomorrow: let me live tonight!

Othello   Nay, if you strive –

100 **Desdemona**   But half an hour!

Othello   Being done, there is no pause.

Desdemona   But while I say one prayer!

Desdemona   He found it then. I never gave it to him. Send for him here. Let him admit the truth.

Othello   He has admitted it.

Desdemona   What, my lord?

Othello   That he has had his way with you.

Desdemona   How do you mean? Adulterously?

Othello   Yes.

Desdemona   He would not say so!

Othello   No. His mouth is shut. Honest Iago has seen to that.

Desdemona   I fear the worst, then. What, is he dead?

Othello   Had all his hairs been lives, my great revenge could cope with all of them.

Desdemona   Alas, he's done for, and I am ruined! [*She bursts into tears*]

Othello   You strumpet! Are you crying for him to my face?

Desdemona   Oh, banish me, my lord, but do not kill me!

Othello   [*pushing her fiercely*] Down, strumpet!

Desdemona   Kill me tomorrow! Let me live tonight!

Othello   If you struggle –

Desdemona   Just half an hour!

Othello   There's no stopping now!

Desdemona   Just while I say one prayer!

Othello   It is too late.

Desdemona   Oh Lord, Lord, Lord!

[*He smothers her*]

105 **Emilia**   [*within*] My lord, my lord! What, ho! My lord, my
lord!

Othello   What voice is this? Not dead? Not yet quite
dead?
I, that am cruel, am yet merciful:
110 I would not have thee linger in thy pain.
So, so.

Emilia   [*within*] What, ho; my lord, my lord!

Othello   Who's there?

Emilia   [*within*] Oh, good my lord, I'd speak a word with
115 you!

Othello   Yes, 'tis Emilia. By and by! She's dead.
'Tis like she comes to speak of Cassio's death:
The noise was high. Ha; no more moving.
Still as the grave. Shall she come in? Were't good?
120 I think she stirs again. No. What's best to do?
If she come in, she'll sure speak to my wife.
My wife! My wife! What wife! I have no wife.
Oh, insupportable! Oh, heavy hour!
Methinks it should be now a huge eclipse
125 Of sun and moon, and that the affrighted globe
Should yawn at alteration.

Emilia   [*within*] I do beseech you
That I may speak with you. Oh, good my lord!

Othello   It is too late. [*He seizes a pillow*]

Desdemona   Oh Lord, Lord, Lord!

[**Othello** *smothers her*]

Emilia   [*from outside*] My lord, my lord! Hello! My lord, my lord!

Othello   Who's voice was that? [**Desdemona** *is still moving feebly*] Not dead? Not yet completely dead? Cruel I am – but merciful, too. I would not have you lingering in pain. [*He presses the pillow down again*] So, so.

Emilia   My lord, my lord!

Othello   Who's there?

Emilia   Oh, good my lord! Can I have a word with you?

Othello   Yes, it's Emilia. [*Calling*] In a minute. [*He removes the pillow*] She's dead. She's no doubt come to tell me about Cassio's death: she sounded excited. [*He checks again*] Ha! Quite still? Still as the grave . . . Shall I let her in? Would that be wise? [*Looking at* **Desdemona**] I think she moved again . . . No. What's the best thing to do? If she comes in, she's sure to speak to my wife . . . My wife! My wife! What wife? I have no wife! Oh, it's unbearable! Oh, grief! A huge eclipse of the sun and moon should happen now, I think, and earth should quake in fear and split asunder.

Emilia   Please, I must speak to you! Oh, good my lord!

Othello   I had forgot thee. Oh, come in, Emilia.
130   Soft; by and by. Let me the curtains draw.
      Where art thou? [*He unlocks door*] What's the matter
      with thee now?

[*Enter* **Emilia**]

Emilia   Oh, my good lord, yonder's foul murder done.

Othello   What; now?

135 **Emilia**   But now, my lord.

Othello   It is the very error of the moon;
      She comes more nearer earth than she was wont,
      And makes men mad.

Emilia   Cassio, my lord, hath killed a young Venetian
140   Called Roderigo.

Othello   Roderigo killed?
      And Cassio killed?

Emilia   No, Cassio is not killed.

Othello   Not Cassio killed? Then murder's out of tune,
145   And sweet revenge grows harsh.

Desdemona   Oh, falsely, falsely murdered!

Emilia   Oh Lord; what cry is that?

Othello   That? What?

Emilia   Out and alas, that was my lady's voice!

[*She draws back the curtains*]

150   Help, help, ho, help! Oh, lady, speak again!
      Sweet Desdemona, oh sweet mistress, speak!

Desdemona   A guiltless death I die.

Emilia   Oh, who has done this deed?

Othello   I'd forgotten you. Come in, Emilia. But just a moment. Let me draw the curtains. [*He hides* **Desdemona's** *body*] Where are you? [*He unlocks the door*] What's the matter with you now?

[**Emilia** *enters*]

Emilia   Oh, my good lord! There's been a terrible murder!

Othello   What? Now?

Emilia   Just now, my lord.

Othello   It's the moon's fault: she's nearer earth than usual, and making men mad.

Emilia   My lord, Cassio has killed a young Venetian called Roderigo.

Othello   Roderigo killed? And Cassio killed?

Emilia   No, my lord. Cassio hasn't been killed.

Othello   Cassio not killed? Then murder's gone wrong, and sweet revenge is frustrated.

Desdemona   [*from behind the curtains*] Oh, wrongly, wrongly murdered!

Emilia   Oh Lord! Who said that?

Othello   That? What?

Emilia   Alas, that was my lady's voice!

[*She draws back the curtain*]

Help, help, oh help! Oh, lady, say something! Sweet Desdemona, oh, sweet mistress, speak!

Desdemona   I die in innocence.

Emilia   Oh, who did this to you?

267

Desdemona   Nobody – I myself – farewell.
155   Commend me to my kind lord – Oh, farewell!

[*She dies*]

Othello   Why, how should she be murdered?

Emilia   Alas, who knows?

Othello   You heard her say herself it was not I.

Emilia   She said so. I must needs report the truth.

160 **Othello**   She's like a liar gone to burning hell:
'Twas I that killed her.

Emilia   Oh, the more angel she,
And you the blacker devil!

Othello   She turned to folly, and she was a whore.

165 **Emilia**   Thou dost belie her, and thou art a devil.

Othello   She was false as water.

Emilia   Thou art rash as fire
To say that she was false. Oh, she was heavenly true!

Othello   Cassio did top her: ask thy husband else.
170   Oh, I were damned beneath all depth in hell
But that I did proceed upon just grounds
To this extremity. Thy husband knew it all.

Emilia   My husband?

Othello   Thy husband.

175 **Emilia**   That she was false to wedlock?

Othello   Aye, with Cassio. Had she been true,
If heaven would make me such another world
Of one entire and perfect chrysolite,
I'd not have sold her for it.

Desdemona   Nobody. I did it myself. Farewell. My respects to my kind lord. Oh, farewell!

[*She dies*]

Othello   Why, how could she have been murdered?

Emilia   Alas, who knows?

Othello   You heard her say herself it wasn't me.

Emilia   That's what she said. I must report the truth.

Othello   Like the liar she is, she's gone to hell fire. I killed her!

Emilia   Oh, the more she is an angel, and you the blacker devil!

Othello   She turned promiscuous. She was a whore!

Emilia   You slander her. You are a devil!

Othello   She was as treacherous as water!

Emilia   And you're as rash as fire to say so! Oh, she was divinely loyal!

Othello   Cassio slept with her: ask your husband if you doubt it. Oh, if I hadn't proceeded on just grounds to this extreme, I'd be damned to the uttermost depths of hell! Your husband knew all about it.

Emilia   My husband?

Othello   Your husband.

Emilia   That she committed adultery?

Othello   Yes, with Cassio. Had she been faithful, I would not have sold her for a topaz the size of the world.

180 **Emilia**

My husband!

Othello   Ay, 'twas he that told me on her first. An honest
man he is, and hates the slime that sticks on filthy
deeds.

Emilia   My husband!

185 **Othello**   What needs this iterance, woman? I say thy
husband.

Emilia   Oh mistress, villainy hath made mocks with love!
My husband say that she was false?

Othello   He, woman;
190   I say thy husband. Dost understand the word?
My friend, thy husband, honest, honest Iago.

Emilia   If he say so, may his pernicious soul
Rot half a grain a day! He lies to the heart.
She was too fond of her most filthy bargain.

195 **Othello**   Ha!

Emilia   Do thy worst.
This deed of thine is no more worthy heaven
Than thou wast worthy her.

Othello   Peace, you were best.

200 **Emilia**   Thou hast not half that power to do me harm
As I have to be hurt. Oh gull! Oh dolt!
As ignorant as dirt! Thou hast done a deed –
I care not for thy sword – I'll make thee known,
Though I lost twenty lives. Help, help, oh, help!
205   The Moor has killed my mistress. Murder! Murder!

[*Enter* **Montano, Gratiano,** *and* **Iago**]

Montano   What is the matter? How now, General?

Emilia My husband?

Othello Yes, he first told me about it. He's an honest man, and hates the slime of promiscuity.

Emilia My HUSBAND!

Othello Why do you keep repeating yourself, woman? I said 'your husband'.

Emilia Oh, mistress! Villainy has made a mockery of love! Did my husband say she was unfaithful?

Othello He did, woman. I said 'your husband'. Do you understand the word? My friend . . . your husband . . . honest, honest Iago.

Emilia If he said that, may his pernicious soul rot half a grain a day! He lies through his teeth. She was too much in love with her vile husband!

Othello [*reaching for his sword*] Ha!

Emilia Do your worst! What you have done is no more worthy of heaven than you were worthy of her.

Othello Hold your tongue, if you know what's good for you.

Emilia You haven't half the power to hurt me as I have to endure. You credulous fool! You dolt! Pig-ignorant, you've done a deed – [**Othello** *raises his sword*] I'm not frightened of your sword. I'll tell everyone about you if it costs me twenty lives. [*She goes to the door*] Help, help, oh help! The Moor has killed my mistress! Murder, murder!

[**Montano, Gratiano, Iago** *and others enter*]

Montano What's going on? What's all this, General?

271

Emilia   Oh, are you come, Iago? You have done well,
That men must lay their murders on your neck.

Gratiano   What is the matter?

210 **Emilia**   Disprove this villain, if thou be'st a man.
He says thou told'st him that his wife was false.
I know thou didst not; thou art not such a villain.
Speak for my heart is full.

Iago   I told him what I thought, and told no more.
215   Than what he found himself was apt and true.

Emilia   But did you ever tell him she was false?

Iago   I did.

Emilia   You told a lie, an odious damned lie!
Upon my soul, a lie, a wicked lie!
220   She false with Cassio! Did you say with Cassio?

Iago   With Cassio, mistress! Go to, charm your tongue.

Emilia   I will not charm my tongue; I am bound to speak:
My mistress here lies murdered in her bed.

All   Oh heavens forfend!

225 **Emilia**   And your reports have set the murder on.

Othello   Nay, stare not masters: it is true indeed.

Gratiano   'Tis a strange truth.

Montano   Oh monstrous act!

Emilia   Oh, you've come, Iago? Promotion indeed when men hold you responsible for their murders!

All   What's the matter?

Emilia   [*to* **Iago**] Contradict this villain, if you're a man. He says you told him that his wife was unfaithful. I know you didn't. You're not such a villain. Tell them. I'm too choked.

Iago   I told him what I thought; and told no more than what he discovered for himself was right and true.

Emilia   But did you ever tell him she was unfaithful?

Iago   I did.

Emilia   You told a lie – an odious, damned lie! Upon my soul, a lie, a wicked lie! She have an affair with Cassio? Did you say with Cassio?

Iago   With Cassio, mistress. That's enough. Shut your mouth.

Emilia   I will not shut my mouth! I've got to say my piece. My mistress lies here murdered in her bed!

All   Heaven forbid!

Emilia   [*to* **Iago**] And what you said provoked the murder.

Othello   Don't look surprised, gentlemen. It is true indeed.

Gratiano   A strange truth!

Montano   A monstrous deed!

Emilia   Villainy, villainy, villainy!
230   I think upon't: I think I smell't – Oh villainy!
       I thought so then; I'll kill myself for grief.
       Oh villainy, villainy!

Iago   What, are you mad? I charge you get you home.

Emilia   Good gentlemen, let me have leave to speak.
235   'Tis proper I obey him, but not now.
       Perchance, Iago, I will ne'er go home.

Othello   Oh! Oh! Oh! (*He falls on the bed*)

Emilia   Nay, lay thee down and roar,
       For thou hast killed the sweetest innocent
240   That e'er did lift up eye.

Othello   [*rising*] Oh, she was foul!
       I scarce did know you, uncle. There lies your niece,
       Whose breath indeed these hands have newly stopped.
       I know this act shows horrible and grim.

245 **Gratiano**   Poor Desdemona, I am glad thy father's dead:
       Thy match was mortal to him, and pure grief
       Shore his old thread in twain. Did he live now,
       This sight would make him do a desperate turn,
       Yea, curse his better angel from his side,
250   And fall to reprobation.

Othello   'Tis pitiful: but yet Iago knows
       That she with Cassio hath the act of shame
       A thousand times committed. Cassio confessed it,
       And she did gratify his amorous works
255   With that recognizance and pledge of love
       Which I first gave her. I saw it in his hand:
       It was a handkerchief, an antique token
       My father gave my mother.

Emilia   Oh God! Oh heavenly God!

Emilia   Villainy, villainy, villainy! Let me think. I think I've got it – [*She remembers the handkerchief*] Oh, villainy! I thought so at the time! I'll kill myself from grief! Oh, villainy, villainy!

Iago   Have you gone mad? I order you to go home!

Emilia   Good gentlemen, give me permission to speak. It's right that I should obey him, but not now. Maybe, Iago, I'll never go home again.

Othello   [*falling on the bed*] Oh, oh, oh!

Emilia   Oh yes – lie down and roar! You've killed the sweetest innocent that ever opened her eyes!

Othello   [*rising*] Oh, she was foul! [*To* **Gratiano**] I hardly knew you, uncle. There lies your niece, whom I have just killed with my own hands. I know this deed looks terrible and grim . . .

Gratiano   Poor Desdemona! I'm glad your father is dead. Your marriage was a mortal blow: grief killed him. If he were alive now, this sight would turn his mind. Yes, he'd curse away his guardian angel, and commit himself to hell.

Othello   It's awful; but Iago knows that she and Cassio have fornicated a thousand times. Cassio confessed it, and she rewarded his lovemaking with the love-token which was my first present to her. I saw it in his hand. It was a handkerchief, an heirloom which my father gave my mother.

Emilia   Oh God! Oh God in heaven!

260 **Iago**   Zounds, hold your peace!

Emilia   'Twill out, it will. I hold my peace sir? No.
I'll be in speaking liberal as the air.
Let heaven, and men, and devils, let them all,
All, all cry shame against me, yet I'll speak.

265 **Iago**   Be wise, and get you home.

Emilia   I will not.

[**Iago** *draws his sword*]

Gratiano   Fie!
Your sword upon a woman!

Emilia   Oh thou dull Moor, that handkerchief thou
270   speak'st of
I found by fortune and did give my husband;
For often, with a solemn earnestness –
More than indeed belonged to such a trifle –
He begged of me to steal it.

275 **Iago**   Villainous whore!

Emilia   She give it Cassio? No, alas, I found it
And I did give't my husband.

Iago   Filth, thou liest!

Emilia   By heaven I do not, I do not, gentlemen.
280   Oh murderous coxcomb! What should such a fool
Do with so good a wife?

Othello   Are there no stones in heaven
But what serve for the thunder? Precious villain!

[*He runs at* **Iago**; **Montano** *disarms him*]

[**Iago** *stabs* **Emilia**]

Gratiano   The woman falls; sure he hath killed his wife.

Iago   Dammit, shut your mouth!

Emilia   It will all come out, it will! Me shut my
mouth? No! I'll say what I have to say, as free as
the air. God, and men, and devils — they can all, all
cry shame upon me — but I'll speak!

Iago   Use your wits and get off home.

Emilia   I won't.

[**Iago** *draws his sword*]

Gratiano   What! Threaten a woman with your sword?

Emilia   Oh, you stupid Moor! That handkerchief you
mentioned — I found it by chance, and gave it to my
husband because he'd often begged me to steal it,
with an earnestness out of all proportion to its
value.

Iago   You villainous whore!

Emilia   She give it to Cassio? No, alas. I found it, and
I gave it to my husband.

Iago   Filth! You're lying!

Emilia   By God, I'm not, I'm not, gentlemen. [*To*
Othello] Oh you murderous idiot! What would such
a fool as you be doing with so good a woman?

Othello   [*the truth dawning on him at last*] Are there
no surplus thunderbolts in heaven to punish
wickedness? You scum! [*He runs towards* **Iago**.
Montano *restrains him*. **Iago** *stabs* **Emilia** *and
escapes*]

Gratiano   The woman's injured. He's killed his wife
for sure!

285 **Emilia**   Ay, ay: oh lay me by my mistress' side.

*[Exit **Iago**]*

Gratiano   He's gone, but his wife's killed.

Montano   'Tis a notorious villain. Take you this weapon,
Which I have here recovered from the Moor.
Come guard the door without. Let him not pass,
290   But kill him rather. I'll after that same villain,
For 'tis a damned slave.

*[Exeunt **Montano** and **Gratiano**]*

Othello   I am not valiant neither,
But every puny whipster gets my sword.
But why should honour outlive honesty?
295   Let it go all.

Emilia   What did thy song bode, lady?
Hark, canst thou hear me? I will play the swan,
And die in music. *[Singing] Willow, willow, willow.*
Moor, she was chaste; she loved thee, cruel Moor,
300   So come my soul to bliss, as I speak true;
So speaking as I think, I die, I die.

[She dies]

Othello   I have another weapon in this chamber:
It is a sword of Spain, the ice-brook's temper.
Oh, here it is. Uncle, I must come forth.

305 **Gratiano**   *[within]* If thou attempt it, it will cost thee dear;
Thou hast no weapon, and perforce must suffer.

Othello   Look in upon me then, and speak to me,
Or naked as I am I will assault thee.

*[Enter **Gratiano**]*

Emilia   Yes, yes. Lay me beside my mistress.

Gratiano   He's gone, but his wife's been killed.

Montano   He's an out-and-out scoundrel. Take this weapon which I've taken from the Moor. Guard the outside door. Don't let him through. Kill him if necessary. I'll chase that villain. He's a damned rogue.

[**Montano** and **Gratiano** rush off]

Othello   I am a coward, too. Any little whippersnapper can take my sword. But why should reputation remain when honour is lost? Let it all go!

Emilia   What did your song foretell, lady? Listen, can you hear me? I'll sing you the swan song. [She sings] Willow, willow, willow . . . Moor, she was chaste. She loved you, cruel Moor. So may my soul be saved, since I speak the truth. So, speaking my mind, I die, I die . . .

[She dies]

Othello   I have another weapon in this room. It's a Spanish sword with a keen edge. [He looks for it] Oh, here it is. [Calling] Uncle, I must come out!

Gratiano   [outside] Try it, and you'll be sorry. You have no weapon and you'll get hurt.

Othello   Come inside to me, then, and speak to me – or I'll take you on unarmed.

[**Gratiano** enters the room]

Gratiano   What is the matter?

310 **Othello**   Behold, I have a weapon:
A better never did itself sustain
Upon a soldier's thigh. I have seen the day
That with this little arm and this good sword,
I have made my way through more impediments
315 Than twenty times your stop. But, oh vain boast! –
Who can control his fate? 'Tis not so now.
Be not afraid, though you do see me weaponed:
Here is my journey's end; here is my butt
And very sea-mark of my utmost sail.
320 Do you go back dismayed? 'Tis a lost fear:
Man but a rush against Othello's breast,
And he retires. Where should Othello go?
Now: how dost thou look now? Oh ill-starred wench;
Pale as thy smock! When we shall meet at count,
325 This look of thine will hurl my soul from heaven
And fiends will snatch at it. Cold, cold, my girl,
Even like thy chastity. Oh, cursed slave!
Whip me, you devils,
From the possession of this heavenly sight!
330 Blow me about in winds! Roast me in sulphur!
Wash me in steep-down gulfs of liquid fire!
Oh Desdemona! Dead Desdemona! Dead! Oh! Oh!

[*Enter* **Lodovico, Cassio** *in a chair,* **Montano** *and officers*
with **Iago**, *prisoner*]

Lodovico   Where is this rash and most unfortunate man?

Othello   That's he that was Othello. Here I am.

335 **Lodovico**   Where is that viper? Bring the villain forth.

Gratiano   What do you want?

Othello   [*showing his sword*] See – I have a weapon!
No better ever hung from a soldier's belt. I've seen
the day when – with this little arm and this good
sword – I've fought my way through more
opposition than twenty times your might. But what
an empty boast. Who is master of his own fate? It's
not so now . . . Don't be afraid, armed though I am.
My life's journey ends here. Here is my final
destination, the terminus of my last voyage. Do you
draw back in fear? There is no need. Push a mere
reed against his chest, and Othello will retreat.
Where would Othello go? [*He turns to* **Desdemona**]
Now. How do you look now? Oh, ill-fated girl, pale
as your nightdress. When we meet on judgement
day, this look of yours will hurl my soul from
heaven, and fiends will snatch at it. [*He touches her
face*] Cold, cold my girl; just like your chastity. [*Self-
reproach overcomes him*] Oh, you cursed villain!
Whip me, you devils, out of this heavenly sight!
Blow me about in winds! Roast me in sulphur!
Dowse me in cascades of liquid fire! Oh,
Desdemona! Dead Desdemona! Dead! Oh, oh, oh!

[**Lodovico** *and* **Montano** *enter, followed by* **Iago**
under guard, and **Cassio***, who is carried in on a
stretcher*]

Lodovico   Where is this rash and most unfortunate
man?

Othello   He who was Othello . . . here I am.

Lodovico   [*gesturing to his prisoner*] Where is that
viper? Bring him forward.

[**Iago** *is brought face to face with* **Othello**]

Othello   I look down towards his feet; but that's a fable.
If that thou be'st a devil, I cannot kill thee.

[*He wounds* **Iago**]

Lodovico   Wrench his sword from him.

Iago   I bleed, sir, but not killed.

340 **Othello**   I am not sorry neither. I'd have thee live,
For in my sense 'tis happiness to die.

Lodovico   Oh, thou Othello, that wast once so good,
Fallen in the practice of a cursed slave,
What shall be said to thee?

345 **Othello**   Why, anything;
An honourable murderer, if you will:
For naught I did in hate, but all in honour.

Lodovico   This wretch hath part confessed his villainy.
Did you and he consent in Cassio's death?

350 **Othello**   Ay.

Cassio   Dear General, I never gave you cause.

Othello   I do believe it, and I ask your pardon.
Will you, I pray, demand that demi-devil
Why he hath thus ensnared my soul and body?

355 **Iago**   Demand me nothing. What you know, you know.
From this time forth I never will speak word.

Lodovico   What, not to pray?

Gratiano   Torments will ope your lips.

Othello   Well, thou dost best.

Othello [*recalling the belief that devils have cloven hoofs*] I look down at his feet: but that's a fairy-story. If you are a devil, I cannot kill you!

[*He lunges at* **Iago**, *and wounds him*]

Lodovico Get his sword!

Iago I'm wounded, sir, but not killed.

Othello Nor am I sorry. I want you to live. As I see it, it's happiness to die.

Lodovico Oh, Othello – who was once so good – disgraced through the trickery of a damned scoundrel! What can one say to you?

Othello Why, anything. 'An honourable murderer', if you like. I did nothing out of hatred. Honour was my sole motive.

Lodovico [*nodding towards* **Iago**] This wretch has partly confessed his villainy. Did you and he conspire in the attempt on Cassio's life?

Othello Yes.

Cassio Dear General – I never gave you cause!

Othello I quite believe it, and I ask your pardon. Will you ask that demi-devil why he has entrapped my soul and my body in this way?

Iago Ask me nothing. What you know, you know. From now on I will not say a word.

Lodovico What, not even to pray?

Gratiano Torture will open your lips!

Othello Well, that's best.

360 **Lodovico**   Sir, you shall understand what hath befallen,
     Which as I think, you know not. Here is a letter
     Found in the pocket of the slain Roderigo,
     And here another. The one of them imports
     The death of Cassio, to be undertook
365 By Roderigo.

     Othello   Oh villain!

     Cassio   Most heathenish and most gross!

     Lodovico   Now here's another discontented paper
     Found in his pocket too; and this, it seems
370 Roderigo meant to have sent this damned villain,
     But that, belike, Iago, in the nick,
     Came in and satisfied him.

     Othello   Oh the pernicious caitiff!
     How came you, Cassio, by that handkerchief
375 That was my wife's?

     Cassio   I found it in my chamber;
     And he himself confessed but even now
     That there he dropped it for a special purpose
     Which wrought to his desire.

380 **Othello**   Oh fool, fool, fool!

     Cassio   There is besides in Roderigo's letter
     How he upbraids Iago, that he made him
     Brave me upon the watch, whereon it came
     That I was cast; and even but now he spake
385 After long seeming dead, Iago hurt him,
     Iago set him on.

     Lodovico   You must forsake this room and go with us.
     Your power and your command is taken off
     And Cassio rules in Cyprus. For this slave,
390 If there be any cunning cruelty

Lodovico   Sir, you must learn what's happened, since I think you do not know. Here is a letter, found in the pocket of the murdered Roderigo. And here's another. One of them proposes that Cassio should be killed, with Roderigo the assassin.

Othello   Oh, the villain!

Cassio   So barbaric and so monstrous!

Lodovico   Now here's another distasteful document, also found in his pocket. It seems Roderigo meant to send it to this damned villain, except that Iago probably arrived before he did, and put his mind at rest.

Othello   Oh, the wicked wretch! Cassio, how did you obtain my wife's handkerchief?

Cassio   I found it in my room. Iago has confessed that he planted it there for his own special purposes.

Othello   [*beating his breast*] Oh fool, fool, fool!

Cassio   Roderigo's letter also reproaches Iago for making him pick a fight with me when I was on duty, which was the cause of my demotion. And just now – after seeming to be dead for some time – he spoke, saying that Iago injured him and Iago told him what to do.

Lodovico   [*to* **Othello**] You must quit this room and go with us. You are relieved of your command. Cassio is now the Governor of Cyprus. [*To* **Iago**] As for this wretch, his punishment shall be as long and

That can torment him much, and hold him long,
It shall be his. You shall close prisoner rest,
Till that the nature of your fault be known
To the Venetian state. Come, bring him away.

395 **Othello**   Soft you; a word or two before you go.
I have done the state some service and they know't:
No more of that. I pray you in your letters
When you shall these unlucky deeds relate
Speak of me as I am: nothing extenuate,
400 Nor set down aught in malice. Then must you speak
Of one that loved not wisely, but too well;
Of one, not easily jealous, but being wrought,
Perplexed in the extreme; of one whose hand,
Like the base Indian, threw a pearl away
405 Richer than all his tribe; of one whose subdued eyes,
Albeit unused to the melting mood,
Drop tears as fast as the Arabian trees
Their medicinal gum. Set you down this:
And say, besides, that in Aleppo once
410 Where a malignant and a turbaned Turk
Beat a Venetian and traduced the state,
I took by the throat the circumcised dog
And smoke him thus.

[*He stabs himself*]

Lodovico   Oh bloody period!

415 **Gratiano**   All that's spoke is marred!

Othello   I kissed thee ere I killed thee: no way but this,
Killing myself, to die upon a kiss.

[*He falls on the bed and dies*]

Cassio   This did I fear, but thought he had no weapon,
For he was great of heart.

lingering a death as can be devised. [*To* **Othello**]
You will be under close arrest till your offence is
reported to the Venetian state. Take him away!

Othello   One moment. A word or two before you go. I
have served the state well, and they know it.
Enough of that. I would ask you, in your letters
describing these unfortunate deeds, to describe me
as I am. Excuse nothing, nor write down anything in
malice. And you must speak of a man who loved
not wisely, but too well; of one who was not
naturally jealous, but who, being worked upon, was
tormented in the extreme; of one who, like an
ignorant savage, threw away a priceless pearl; of
one whose weeping eyes – though unused to
crying – shed tears as copiously as Arabian trees
ooze myrrh. Write this down, and add that once, in
Aleppo where a vicious turbanned Turk thrashed a
Venetian and insulted the state, I took the
circumcised dog by the throat, and struck him like
this –

[**Othello** *snatches his dagger from its sheath and
stabs himself*]

Lodovico   Oh, what a gory end!

Gratiano   Words are inadequate.

Othello   [*To* **Desdemona**] I kissed you before I killed
you. Killing myself, there's no alternative but to die
upon a kiss . . .

[*He falls on the bed, and dies*]

Cassio   I feared this might happen, but thought he
had no weapon. He was so great of heart.

420 **Lodovico**   [*to* **Iago**]   Oh Spartan dog,
More fell than anguish, hunger, or the sea:
Look on the tragic loading of this bed.
This is thy work. The object poisons sight;
Let it be hid. Gratiano, keep the house
425 And seize upon the fortunes of the Moor,
For they succeed on you. To you, Lord Governor,
Remains the censure of this hellish villain:
The time, the place, the torture. Oh, enforce it!
Myself will straight aboard, and to the state
430 This heavy act with heavy heart relate.

[*Exeunt*]

Lodovico   [*To* **Iago**] You savage dog! More fearsome
than suffering, hunger, or the sea! Look at the tragic
burden of this bed! This is your work. It blinds the
eye: conceal it. Gratiano, take charge of the house
and seize the Moor's fortune, for it is now yours.
[*To* **Cassio**] Lord Governor, the punishment of this
hellish villain is left to you: the time, the place, the
torture. See it is done! I myself will sail
immediately, and with a heavy heart relate this
grievous story to the State.

[*They go*]

Activities

Characters

Search the text to find answers to the following questions.
They will help you to form personal opinions about the
major characters in the play. Record any relevant
quotations in Shakespeare's own words.

Othello

1   We learn a good deal about Othello before he appears.
    Find textual evidence for the following from *Act 1
    Scene 1*:
    a he is a Moor
    b he is subject to racial prejudice
    c he is a commander who makes his own decisions
    d he is articulate
    e he has enemies
    f he is indispensable to Venice.
    Why do you think Shakespeare delays Othello's
    entrance until *Act 1 Scene 2*?

2   How do we know from *Act 1 Scene 2* that Othello is:
    a proud
    b authoritative
    c self-made
    d of royal blood
    e in love?

3   In *Act 1 Scene 3*, whilst defending himself against
    Brabantio's charge of witchcraft, Othello says:
    a He lacks eloquence. Is this true?

b He is a soldier. What do we know of his military episodes?

c He has travelled widely. What do we learn of his experiences?

Othello's account of his courtship is later described as 'bragging' (Iago, *Act 2 Scene 1*). Do you think it is?

4 Later in *Act 1 Scene 3*, Othello denies that he is motivated by physical passion, and claims that he will never let his private life affect his professional conduct.

   a Find the relevant lines, and decide whether (in the light of subsequent events) Othello's self-esteem is justified.

   b Read Iago's soliloquy at the end of Act 1 and:

     i note the alleged flaw in Othello's character

     ii check it against Othello's actual behaviour.

Is this weakness in Othello a virtue or a vice?

5 In *Act 2 Scene 1*, Iago identifies four defects in Othello which, he says, will eventually cause Desdemona to be unfaithful to him. He also identifies four virtues.

   a List all eight.

   b Say which are related to Othello's personality, and which are those over which he has no control.

6 In *Act 2 Scene 3*, Othello speaks of his 'best judgement' being 'collied'. (Read the modern translation if this is not clear to you).

   a What causes this?

   b Where else in the play does Othello's judgement fail him?

7 In *Act 3 Scene 3*, Iago's threat to 'pour this pestilence into his ear' causes Othello to change from dotage ('Perdition catch my soul but I do love thee') to thoughts of murder ('Damn her, lewd minx! Oh, damn her!') This happens in stages.

   a The key words in the first stage are 'think' and

'thought'. Find the lines which cause Othello to rise to Iago's bait, and decide whether the Moor asks for what he gets.

b The next words to note are 'seem' and 'seeming'. Find the lines where they occur, and consider whether Othello is naive in assuming Iago is an honest man.

c Thirdly, the word 'jealousy' is voiced. Find Iago's first three uses of the word, and then explain how the repetition leads to Othello's speech ending 'Away at once with love or jealousy!'

d Immediately afterwards Othello relapses into a series of brief responses. How many of these are there, and what do you think is the reason for their brevity?

e Left alone, Othello speaks his thoughts aloud. Find examples of;
  i self pity
  ii hurt pride
  iii naivety
in the speech beginning 'This fellow's of exceeding honesty'.

f On his return after the handkerchief episode, Othello shows that he now accepts Iago's slanders as fact. Find the lines which confirm this, then identify examples of his
  i emotional instability
  ii brooding introspection
  iii passionate self-pity
  iv mental confusion
  v homicidal anger.
Do you agree with Iago when he says Othello is 'eaten up with passion'?

g At this point in the scene, Iago's language coarsens, and Othello is again reduced to simple exclamations.

Finally he exclaims 'Oh that the slave had forty thousand lives!'

    i Which of Othello's words show that Iago's manipulations have succeeded?

    ii Which words indicate that Othello has decided to act?

    iii Which words and actions in the last twenty lines of the scene are reminiscent of the marriage ceremony?

8 In *Act 3 Scene 4*, Othello begins by addressing Desdemona with cold politeness, and exits uttering an oath.

  a Trace the stages leading up to this angry climax.

  b Explain how Othello's rising anger is revealed in his exclamations.

9 In *Act 4 Scene 1*, Iago returns to the issue of the handkerchief.

  a How do we know from Othello's words and subsequent epileptic fit that he attaches major importance to it?

  b Do you agree with Iago that Othello's display of 'grief' is 'A passion most unsuiting such a man'?

  c Is Othello's subsequent role as an eavesdropper equally 'unsuiting'?

10 Othello's mental torment is evident in the rest of the scene.

  a How is it revealed after Cassio's departure?

  b How does it show during and after his reading of the letter from Venice?

  c How can we tell from his last three words that seeds planted by Iago in *Act 3 Scene 3* have taken root?

11 *Act 4 Scene 2* has been called 'the brothel scene', because Othello treats Emilia as if she were a maid serving a prostitute.

    a Find the words which account for this description.

    b Read the speech beginning 'Had it pleased Heaven', and say whether there is evidence in it of hurt pride and vanity.

12 In *Act 5 Scene 2*, Othello murders Desdemona.

    a Demonstrate from his opening speech that his love for her remains.

    b What outward signs of his internal passion are noted by Desdemona?

    c What are the two 'facts' which Othello cites in evidence against her?

    d What is his way of showing that though he is cruel, he is nevertheless merciful?

13 After the murder, Othello's behaviour has many facets. How does he show:

    a indecision

    b fear

    c self-pity

    d guilt

    e prevarication?

    Which is the line that tells us that Othello has finally understood the truth?

14 In his words and deeds before his death, Othello exhibits several changes of character.

    a He admits to a 'vain boast'. What is it?

    b He loses his soldier's instinct for self defence. In what way?

    c He suffers remorse. Find two lines that confirm this.

15 Othello dies rather than be taken prisoner.

    a Show how his last moments contain elements of pride

    b Decide whether he really was

      i 'one that loved not wisely but too well'

      ii 'one not easily jealous'.

Iago

1 Iago's character begins to emerge as soon as the
   curtain rises on *Act 1*. Find evidence to show he is:
   a deceitful
   b ambitious
   c envious
   d proud of his professionalism
   e devious
   f governed by self-interest
   g a trouble-maker
   h foul-mouthed.

2 With Othello in *Act 1 Scene 1* Iago's duplicity is shown
   in action. How does he pretend he has:
   a moral standards
   b a loyal streak
   c a caring manner?

3 In *Act 1 Scene 3*, Iago is alone again with Roderigo.
   What do we learn:
   a about his age
   b his moral philosophy
   c his cynicism?

4 After Roderigo goes, what do we discover from Iago's
   soliloquy about:
   a his suspicious nature
   b his unscrupulousness
   c his cunning
   d his evil tendencies?
   What is the evidence here to suggest that Iago's
   scheming is primarily against Cassio?

5 In *Act 2 Scene 1*, Iago has reached Cyprus safely. Show
   how he can be:
   a amusing
   b witty
   in the presence of ladies, but

    c coarse
    d malevolent
    with his enemies.

6 By now, the word 'honest' is attaching itself to Iago in that he is universally regarded as a man of integrity. Collect as many examples of these flattering references to him as you can find throughout the play.

7 When alone with Roderigo, however, the real Iago emerges. Show how
    a his lying
    b his contempt for women
    c his contempt for men
    d his manipulative skills
    are revealed in *Act 2 Scene 1*.

8 In the soliloquy that follows, Iago's plan develops.
    a How do we know he believes his own lies?
    b How do we know he finds Desdemona attractive?
    c How do we know he suspects the Moor of adultery with Emilia?
    d How do we know he has not yet worked out a full plan of campaign?
    At what point in this speech does the scheme to make Othello jealous come into his mind?

9 The plot to ruin Cassio is carried out in *Act 2 Scene 3*.
    a Explain how he manipulates Cassio.
    b Explain what role Roderigo is expected to play.
    c Explain how he brings about Cassio's downfall by pretending to be his friend
      i when speaking to Othello
      ii when giving advice to Cassio himself.
    d Explain how in his soliloquy near the end of the scene Iago shows he is no longer 'confused', but evilly satisfied his plot has taken shape.

10 *Act 3 Scene 3* is notable for Iago's insidious poisoning of Othello's mind. In the first part of this long scene:

   a How does he contrive to blacken Cassio's reputation?

   b How does he make it appear that he speaks his thoughts reluctantly?

   c How does he make it seem that he is a man of honour and integrity?

   d How does he plant the idea of jealousy while appearing to deplore the idea of it?

   e How does he succeed in casting suspicion on Desdemona?

   f How does he undermine Othello's confidence in himself?

   g How does he advance his plots by appearing to advocate constraint?

   h Which line spoken by Iago echoes the warning given to Othello by Brabantio in a rhyming couplet in *Act 1 Scene 3*?

11 Later in the same scene (after Othello's departure) Iago has the good fortune to acquire Desdemona's handkerchief, giving him a further opportunity to poison the Moor's 'sweet sleep'.

   a How do we know the idea of procuring it is not new?

   b In what sense is it 'a trifle light as air', and how is Iago proved right about its significance to Othello?

12 In the last part of this scene, (after Othello's return), Iago achieves his object.

   a Find the lines, spoken as Othello enters, which confirm this.

   b At this point, who does most of the talking?

   c Why is Iago's self-rebuke so effective in fuelling Othello's jealousy?

   d How does Iago intensify it by introducing explicit reference to sex?

e How does he turn the screw with the help of the newly-acquired handkerchief?

Describe how the scene ends with Iago's objectives achieved.

13 Iago's pressure is relentless. In *Act 4 Scene 1*, show how he plays upon Othello's sensitivities by means of:
a references to physical love
b references to the handkerchief
c innuendo.

What does he call his evil practices?

14 a In the same scene, show
   i how he manipulates Cassio; then
   ii how he manipulates Othello
so as to achieve agreement about the murders of Desdemona and Cassio.
b Illustrate how Iago becomes a double-dealer in the final part of the scene.
c Find further evidence of his duplicity in *Act 4 Scene 2*
   i with Desdemona and Emilia and
   ii Roderigo.

15 *Act 5 Scene 1* begins with the attempted murder of Cassio.
a i How has Iago contrived to get Roderigo to do the killing?
   ii Why does Iago think he is in a 'no lose' situation?
   iii Which of the two reasons for Cassio's death sheds most light on Iago's own character?
   iv How does Iago finish off what Roderigo begins?
b The scene continues with the death of Roderigo.
   i How does Iago make it appear that he is on the side of justice?
   ii How does he conceal his guilt?

    iii Give examples of his apparent sympathy for his victim.

    iv Explain how he attempts to implicate Bianca.

16 In the final scene of the play (*Act 5 Scene 2*), Iago is unmasked.

    a Show how his villainy surprises even his wife.

    b Trace his mounting fear of disclosure up to the stabbing of Emilia.

    c Explain why Othello thinks Iago cannot be killed.

    d What is Iago's tactic when his evil is exposed?

    e What is the punishment Lodovico proposes?

Coleridge spoke of Iago's 'motiveless malignity'. Some critics regard this as an over-simplification. What is your opinion?

Desdemona

1 From *Act 1 Scene 1*:

    a Find the lines which show that Roderigo has been trying unsuccessfully to marry Desdemona.

    b Ascertain some of her qualities from what he says about her.

2 What does her father tell us about her in *Act 1 Scene 2?*

3 **a** What more do we learn of her character from Othello in *Act 1 Scene 3?*

    b What can be deduced from her own words in the same scene?

    c What is the contrasting view expressed by Iago?

    d What is Cassio's opinion of her qualities as voiced in *Act 2 Scene 1?*

4 **a** On her arrival in Cyprus, (*Act 2 Scene 1*), Desdemona exchanges pleasantries with Iago as she awaits Othello. How do we know that this is not a sign of shallow indifference to her husband's safety?

b Later in the scene, Iago interprets her character in his own cynical way, both in his prose speeches and in his soliloquy. What does he say of her, and is what he says at all credible?

c What do we learn from the soliloquy of Iago's feelings towards Desdemona?

5 In *Act 2 Scene 3*, Iago speaks to Cassio twice on the subject of Desdemona.

a What is the difference in tone between the two references to her character?

b What adjective does Cassio use to describe her?

c What is Iago's true opinion of Desdemona and her relationship with Othello, as expressed in his soliloquy near the end of the scene?

6 How can we tell from *Act 3 Scene 3* that Desdemona:

a is a loyal friend

b a manipulative wife

c a caring wife?

7 By *Act 3 Scene 4*, Desdemona has lost her handkerchief.

a Why do you think she lies about its loss?

b At what point does she resort to attack as the best form of defence?

c What does she say that demonstrates her willingness to do more for others than she will do for herself?

d How does she make excuses for Othello's behaviour when she might be criticizing it?

8 In *Act 4 Scene 1*, after Othello has descended to eavesdropping, he is tormented by thoughts of Desdemona's apparent vice and undoubted virtues. Find lines to show he believes she is:

a pleasant

b high-class

c gifted

d intelligent.

What other virtues does she show in her response to Othello's harsh words and violence in this scene and the next?

9 Desdemona is under great stress in *Act 4 Scene 2*.

a What line tells us she cannot stand up to chastisement?

b What lines prove her deep love for Othello?

c What lines show her innocence and purity?

What further evidence is there of the latter in *Act 4 Scene 3?*

10 Desdemona is murdered in *Act 5 Scene 2*.

a What 'sins' does she confess to?

b What efforts does she make to save herself?

c What do her dying words tell us of her character?

Emilia

1 Emilia first appears in *Act 2 Scene 1*.

a What does Iago say about her?

b Do you think 'he has little cause to say so'?

2 a What evidence is there in *Act 3 Scene 3* that she is no wiser about her husband's true character than anyone else?

b What does she say of him later in the scene that suggests she knows he has odd ways?

c How do we know she likes to please him?

d How do we know that she has principles?

3 a Emilia is worldly-wise and understands men. Show this from what she says in *Act 3 Scene 4*.

b She is fiercely defensive of Desdemona. Show this from *Act 4 Scene 2*.

    c She has a practical sense of the value of morality.
Show this from *Act 4 Scene 3*.

    d She is a shrewd analyst of husband/wife
relationships. Demonstrate this from her speech at
the end of *Act 4 Scene 3*.

    e She is forthright when there is cause to be. Find
evidence in *Act 5 Scene 1*.

4 This forthrightness is predominant in the part she
plays in *Act 5 Scene 2*.

    a Illustrate how she stands up to Othello.

    b Illustrate how she denounces her husband.

    c Illustrate her reckless disregard for her own safety.
Do you agree with the critic who said 'She rises as
Othello falls?'

Cassio

1 The first impression we have of Michael Cassio is
gained through Iago in *Act 1 Scene 1*.

    a What is this prejudiced view?

    b What Shakespearian error is contained in it?

    c Do you really think Othello was influenced 'by letter
and affection', or is it more likely that he chose the
best man for the job?

2 Cassio speaks for himself in *Act 2 Scene 1*.

    a Demonstrate that he is loyal

    b Demonstrate that he can be fulsome in his praise.

    c Demonstrate that he is socially self-confident.

3 In the same scene, Iago has more slanderous
observations to make about Cassio's character. Sift
these, and extract the elements of truth concerning:

    a Cassio's age

    b his appearance

c his personality.
What ugly suspicions does Iago have of Cassio's
relationship with
   i Desdemona
   ii Emilia?

4 How can we tell from *Act 2 Scene 3* that:
  a Cassio is warmly regarded by Othello
  b that he is loyal and respectful even when his superior
    is not present?
  What do we learn of his 'ingraft infirmity'?

5 After his fall from grace, Cassio is filled with remorse.
  a What grieves him most?
  b Why does he despise himself?
  c How does he become a tool for Iago's evil practices?

6 In *Act 3 Scene 4*, Cassio is with his mistress Bianca.
  a How can we tell that Bianca is in love with him?
  b How is this relationship exploited by Iago in *Act 4
    Scene 1?*
  From what Cassio says to Iago, is Bianca likely ever to
  become his wife?

7 In the last Act:
  a Iago states the reason why Cassio must die. What is
    it?
  b Cassio is wounded. Explain the circumstances.
  c Cassio is promoted. What post is he granted by
    Lodovico?

Roderigo

1 In the Folio edition of the play, Roderigo is described
  as 'a gulled gentleman', that is, one who is deceived
  and duped.
  a How do his first words in the play confirm this?

    b How do his first actions show that he is led on by Iago?

    c How do we know that Brabantio disapproves of him?

2 In *Act 1 Scene 3*, Iago calls him 'a silly gentleman'.

    a Why?

    b What advice is he given?

    c Does he take it?

    In Iago's soliloquy at the end of the scene, what words tell us that Roderigo is held in contempt?

3 In *Act 2 Scene 1*, Roderigo is fed with lies by his mentor Iago.

    a What, to his credit, is Roderigo's first reaction?

    b Iago says 'be ruled by me'. How do we know he is?

    c What is the evidence in Iago's soliloquy to prove that Roderigo is indeed an object of ridicule?

    d How is this further confirmed in Iago's next soliloquy early in *Act 2 Scene 3?*

4 Later in *Act 2 Scene 3*, after Roderigo has been beaten by Cassio, he returns to complain. What words tell us

    a that he realizes he is playing a minor role in events, and

    b that he may end up poorer, sadder and wiser?

5 Roderigo lies low while the main action develops, re-appearing in *Act 4 Scene 2*.

    a What does he say has been Iago's tactic with him in the interval?

    b What signs are there that he has seen through Iago?

    c What more do we learn about how he has 'foolishly suffered'?

    d How does Iago talk him into further involvement?

6 In *Act 5 Scene 1*, Roderigo attempts to kill Cassio.

    a How do we know he is half-hearted in his commitment?

b What euphemism does he use for 'murder'?
c What method has Iago used to incite Roderigo?
d What saves Cassio from Roderigo's sword?

7 **a** Cassio wounds Roderigo. What does the latter say that suggests repentance?
  b Iago stabs Roderigo.
    i What does Roderigo call Iago?
    ii What does Iago call Roderigo?

Textual questions

Read the original Shakespeare and (if necessary) the modern transcription, to gain an understanding of the speeches and extracts below. Then concentrate entirely on the original in answering the questions.

1 *Her father loved me, oft invited me* (Act 1 Scene 3)

  a This is Othello's speech in self-defence against the charge of witchcraft. Why does it begin with three deliberate statements referring to Brabantio's role in the story?

  b How are these three statements balanced by three references to Othello's own career?

  c How does Othello use repetition to sustain interest in his narrative?

  d In describing his 'travels' history', Othello succeeds in giving his listeners both a sense of scale and a sense of terrestrial texture.

    i Which adjective indicates size, and why does its placement after the noun give it an added force?

    ii Which words describe a spacious and daunting landscape?

    iii Which words convey a sense of inhospitable ruggedness?

    iv Which words suggest height?

  e The simple conjunction 'and' links Othello's narrative in a series of fascinating recollections of a life of strange experiences. How is this strangeness conveyed by his use of

    i unusual names

    ii brief explanations?

  f **i** Why do you think Othello takes his narrative so far before referring to Desdemona?

    ii In terms of the imagery used by Othello, why might his words to her be called 'food for thought'?

    iii What part does repetition play in Othello's account of Desdemona's enraptured interest in his life story?

    iv When she says 'she wished that heaven had made her such a man', do you think she means:
'she wished she had been a man such as Othello', or
'she wished heaven had provided such a man for her to love'?

g Explain why Othello and Desdemona loved each other.

h Comment
    i on Othello's use of words of one syllable, and the effectiveness of this;
    ii say whether you consider him to be 'rude in speech' from the evidence of this passage.

2 *Thus do I ever make my fool my purse* (Act 1 Scene 3)

a Some critics have said that the use of the word 'purse' twice within three lines is a Shakespearian oversight. Others think the first line of the soliloquy follows naturally from 'put money enough in your purse', and is Iago's way of saying that in normal circumstances he would be foolish to waste his time talking to a man like Roderigo. Which side of the debate do you support?

b Assuming the latter explanation is the correct one, how does Iago justify his talking to 'a snipe'?

c In this speech, Iago is working out a plan as he goes along. Which words and phrases denote this?

d As part of his 'double knavery', Iago proposes either to 'plume up' his will, or 'make up' his will: the modern translation explains what he means. Editors must make a decision as to which word to use. Consider both, and decide which version appeals to you most.

e What is gained by printing 'As asses are' on a new line?

f The last two lines of the soliloquy rhyme. This can be Shakespeare's way of:

   i indicating the end of a Scene or Act, or

   ii stating something he wishes his audience to note and remember.

In this case, it is the former. Find an example in the play of the latter.

3 *That Cassio loves her I do well believe it* (Act 2 Scene 1)

a Once again Iago is thinking his way forward, speaking his thoughts aloud. Five positive statements are made in the first six lines.

   i Classify them as either true, possibly true, and untrue.

   ii What sixth so-called 'fact' does Iago later add to his list?

b In the line 'If this poor trash of Venice, whom I trash', the word 'trash' (see the translation) is a suggestion by an earlier editor and generally adopted. In the Folio edition, it is 'crush'; in the Quarto, 'trace'; neither of these seems to be right in the context.

   i Do you think a pun is consistent with Iago's character?

   ii Is 'trash' appropriate to the hunting image?

   iii Which of the three words seems best to you?

c Similarly, editors must choose between 'in the rank garb' and 'in the right garb'. The former is the Quarto reading, the latter the Folio. Decide which you prefer bearing these facts in mind:

    i 'Garb' does not mean 'dress', as it does today, but 'way of speaking'.

    ii 'Rank' has also changed its meaning. Whereas it originally meant 'luxuriant of growth', it came to mean 'sexy', or 'lascivious'.

   d Where has Iago used the 'ass' image before?

   e Comment on the reason for the rhyming couplet at the end of the speech.

4 *And what's he then, that says I play the villain?* (Act 2 Scene 3)

   a Do you think the tone of this first line of Iago's soliloquy presupposes an audience? Why might it find his evil amusing?

   b Where else in the speech does Iago excuse his villainy?

   c Where else has Iago referred to Hell in a soliloquy?

   d What do you think 'pitch' means in the phrase 'turn her virtue into pitch':

    i pitch as in 'black as pitch' ie something foul and unclean, or

    ii pitch as a synonym for tar ie something that could be a snare or trap?

   Do the last two lines of the soliloquy influence your decision?

5 *This fellow's of exceeding honesty* (Act 3 Scene 3)

   a In the second sentence of this speech, Othello uses a sustained metaphor. Explain how his willingness to give Desdemona her freedom is related to setting free a wild hawk that has been strapped to its owner's wrist.

   b Consider the reasons he gives for having an unfaithful wife. These are made in private. Are they in accord with Othello's public image?

   c Explain how Othello successfully conveys his horror at the thought of sharing his wife with others.

 d Sometimes even Shakespeare seems illogical or self-contradictory: either he makes a slip of the pen, or what he wrote has been incorrectly transcribed into print. Re-read the sentence beginning 'Yet 'tis the plague of great ones'; then puzzle out:

  i how great ones can suffer more than the base if adultery is a 'destiny unshunnable, like death', and

  ii what Shakespeare meant by 'unshunnable': being destined to be great, or destined to be betrayed by women?

6 *Ay, you did wish that I would make her turn* (Act 4 Scene 1)

This is Othello's response to Lodovico's 'I do beseech your lordship, call her back.'

 a Explain how Othello's repeated use of the word 'turn' conveys both his bitterness and Desdemona's alleged infidelity.

 b What is the effect of his repetition of 'weep'?

 c What is the sinister meaning of 'very' when applied to the thrice-repeated word 'obedient'?

 d Which phrases in this speech would be spoken

  i sarcastically

  ii politely

  iii in anger

  iv like a true commander?

 e Explain the significance of his explosive 'Goats and monkeys!'

7 *Had it pleased heaven to try me with affliction* (Act 4 Scene 2)

 a Can you trace a biblical reference in Othello's reference to suffering through affliction?

 b What three afflictions does he cite?

c What is the rhetorical advantage of Othello's placing the main clause of his first sentence at the end?

d Explain:

  i the clock imagery in his second sentence

  ii the aptness of the reference to 'slow unmoving' fingers.

e How does Othello's series of alternatives convey his passionate sincerity?

f Where has he referred to toads before?

8 *Yes, a dozen, and as many to the vantage as would store the world they played for* (Act 4 Scene 3)

a Why do you think Emilia's speech turns from prose to blank verse?

b Is this another example of a speech deliberately aimed at an audience? If so, explain what may have been Shakespeare's purpose.

c Why is this speech in tune with twentieth-century thinking?

d i List Emilia's accusations against husbands

  ii What claims does she make for wives?

e Explain the purpose of the rhyming couplet which rounds off the speech.

9 *It is the cause, it is the cause, my soul* (Act 5 Scene 2)

a The meaning of the first line of this famous soliloquy has been the subject of much speculation. Does 'cause' mean

  i the cause of justice: Othello's virtuous objective or

  ii Desdemona's alleged adultery?

  Decide which you think Shakespeare intended.

b Some actors stress 'it'; other stress 'cause'. What is the difference, and which do you prefer?

c Similarly, 'Put out the light, and then put out the light'. Much critical ink has been spilled in trying to discover its full meaning.

　　　　i One critic suggested the second 'the' should be
　　　　　'thy'. Comment.
　　　　ii Others recommend a heavy stress on the second
　　　　　'the' when reading the line aloud. Does this help?
　　　　iii Dr Johnson suggested that the second half of the
　　　　　sentence should be a question. Do you agree?
　　d One argument in support of Dr Johnson is that
　　　Othello does proceed to answer a question. Explain
　　　how the use of imagery conveys Othello's meaning.
　　e Show how Othello's use of opposites effectively
　　　expresses the conflict within him.

10 *Soft you, a word or two before you go* (Act 5 Scene 2)
　　a The words 'before you go' do not appear in the
　　　Quarto edition. Decide whether the Folio is, or is
　　　not, more effective.
　　b The Quarto and the Folio disagree about the fifth
　　　line, too. Which do you prefer?
　　　　i 'Speak of them as they are'. (Quarto, meaning the
　　　　　'unlucky deeds') or
　　　　ii 'Speak of me as I am' (Folio)?
　　c How does the repetition of 'of one' four times give
　　　rhetorical strength to Othello's last words?

Examination questions

1 'The faults in Othello's character are such that both he and the play fall short of tragic stature'. Discuss.

2 How successful is Shakespeare in creating (a) an atmosphere of war, and (b) relevant comic interludes in *Othello?*

3 'One that loved not wisely, but too well . . . one not easily jealous'. Is this just, or is Othello guilty of self-delusion?

4 Do you think that Coleridge was right when he spoke of Iago's 'motiveless malignity'?

5 Is the tragedy of Othello traceable to his ethnic origins?

6 Illustrate with as much textual detail as you can how Shakespeare conveys the intensity of Othello's moods and feelings.

7 To what extent is Michael Cassio a victim of (a) 'wine and women', and (b) Iago?

8 It has been said that both Othello's jealousy and the speed with which it develops are unconvincing. Do you agree?

9 '*Othello* is a play in which contrasts of language, character and mood turn melodrama into tragedy'. Discuss.

10 How does Shakespeare present ideas about reputation in *Othello?*

11 Compare and contrast the attitudes to men of the three women characters in *Othello.*

12 Explain why Michael Cassio may be said to justify Iago's description of him as having 'a daily beauty'.

13 How does Shakespeare achieve fast-moving action while at the same time suggesting a more spacious time-scale?

14 Is Desdemona a victim of her own submissive innocence?

15 How do Othello's three soliloquies reveal his state of mind?

16 Discuss and illustrate Shakespeare's use of dramatic irony in *Othello*.

17 Discuss and illustrate the part played by imagery in the dramatic achievement of *Othello*.

18 In his last speech, Othello speaks of 'these unlucky deeds'. Do you think his personal tragedy is caused by bad luck, or bad judgement?

19 To what extent is *Othello* a play about 'appearance and reality'?

20 It has been said that '*Othello* depends for its success on a gullible hero and a gullible audience'. Do you agree?

One-word-answer quiz

1 Towards which island was the Turkish fleet first reported to be sailing?

2 Which island was its destination, according to Signor Angelo?

3 How many ships were in the fleet, according to the highest estimate?

4 How many ships were added to the fleet en route?

5 How many 'lads of Cyprus' conspired to make Cassio drunk?

6 How many times does Othello kiss Desdemona before killing her?

7 How many times afterwards?

8 How many times had Othello fallen into a fit, according to Iago?

9 How old does Iago say he is?

10 How old was Othello when he first went to war?

11 How many letters were found in Roderigo's pocket after his death?

12 For how many hours are the citizens of Cyprus free to celebrate the marriage of Othello and Desdemona?

13 How many important Venetians asked Othello to make Iago his lieutenant?

14 How many fingers did Cassio kiss when speaking to Desdemona at the harbour in Cyprus?

15 What was Iago's military rank at the beginning of the play?

16 What was Brabantio's political rank in Venice?

17 What was the name of Desdemona's mother's maid?

18 What song did this maid die singing?

19 What was the relationship of Gratiano to Brabantio?

20 Of what did Brabantio die, according to Gratiano?

21 What sin does Emilia say she might commit 'for the whole world'?

22 What was the country of origin of the sword used by Othello to commit suicide?

23 What prevents the Turkish fleet from attacking Cyprus?

24 In what kind of tree did a poor soul sit sighing?

25 What does Iago say Roderigo should put in his purse?

26 What was Othello's first gift to Desdemona?

27 What does Roderigo give Iago to further his suit with Desdemona?

28 In what city was Michael Cassio born?

29 What does Cassio bemoan the loss of after his drunken brawling?

30 With what does Othello first plan to kill Desdemona?

31 What fruit was embroidered on Desdemona's handkerchief?

32 Of what material was the handkerchief made?

33 What was used to dye it?

34 Who gave the handkerchief to Othello?

35 Who gave it to this former owner?

36 Who succeeded Othello as Governor of Cyprus?

37 Who was in command of Cyprus before Othello took over?

38 Who, according to Iago, was 'a great arithmetician'?

39 Whose breeches 'cost him but a crown'?

40 Who said he was 'nothing if not critical'?

41 Who does Iago call 'this poor trash of Venice'?

42 For whom would a lady of Venice have walked barefoot to Palestine for one of his kisses?

43 Which sheets does Emilia lay on Desdemona's death-bed?

44 How many men does Iago say he suspects of adultery with his wife?

45 In which part of the body does Iago wound Cassio?

46 With what does he propose to bind the wound?

47 What does he in fact use to stem the flow of blood?

48 What did Othello become after his capture in war?

49 What was to be the destination of Othello and Desdemona – according to Iago – should the former lose his command of Cyprus?

50 What was the length of Cassio's absence from Bianca's house, about which she complains?

What's missing?

Complete the following quotations:

1 Keep up your bright swords, for . . .
2 It is the cause, it is the cause . . .
3 The Moor, howbeit that I endure him not Is . . .
4 Good name in man and woman, dear my lord, Is . . .
5 Farewell to neighing steed, and the shrill trump, The
   . . .
6 My name, that was as fresh As Dian's visage, is . . .
7 Were I the Moor, I would not be Iago: In following
   him . . .
8 Oh, curse of marriage! That we can . . .
9 I do follow here in the chase, not like a hound that
   hunts, but . . .
10 It is impossible you should see this, Were they . . .
11 Dangerous conceits are in their natures poisons, Which
   . . .
12 'Tis true: there's magic in the web of it; A sibyl . . .
13 Look to her, Moor, if thou hast eyes to see: She has
   . . .
14 For of my heart those charms, thine eyes, are blotted:
   . . .
15 Oh perjured woman! Thou dost stone my heart And
   . . .
16 Oh thou weed, that art so lovely fair And smell'st so
   sweet that . . .
17 My mother had a maid called Barbary; She . . .

18 Oh, devil, devil! If that the earth could teem with women's tears . . .

19 And what's he, then, that says I play the villain, When . . .

20 Soft you, a word or two before you go . . .

21 'Tis not a year or two shows us a man. They are . . .

22 Here is my journey's end; here is . . .

23 But jealous souls will not be answered so. They are not . . .

24 Then must you speak of one that . . .

25 Had it pleased heaven to try me with affliction; had he . . .

26 Excellent wretch. Perdition catch my soul But . . .

27 If thou dost slander her, and torture me, Never . . .

28 Was this fair paper, this most goodly book, Made to . . .

29 Let husbands know Their wives . . .

30 Put out the light, and then put out the light: . . .